HALLE BERRY

Recent Titles in Greenwood Biographies

John McCain: A Biography
Elaine S. Povich

Beyoncé Knowles: A Biography
Janice Arenofsky

Jerry Garcia: A Biography
Jacqueline Edmondson

Coretta Scott King: A Biography
Laura T. McCarty

Kanye West: A Biography
Bob Schaller

Peyton Manning: A Biography
Lew Freedman

Miley Cyrus: A Biography
Kimberly Dillon Summers

Ted Turner: A Biography
Michael O'Connor

W. E. B. Du Bois: A Biography
Gerald Horne

George Clooney: A Biography
Joni Hirsch Blackman

Will Smith: A Biography
Lisa M. Iannucci

Toni Morrison: A Biography
Stephanie S. Li

HALLE BERRY

A Biography

Melissa Ewey Johnson

GREENWOOD BIOGRAPHIES

GREENWOOD PRESS
An Imprint of ABC-CLIO, LLC

A B C 🌐 C L I O

Santa Barbara, California • Denver, Colorado • Oxford, England

Copyright 2010 by Melissa Ewey Johnson

Library of Congress Cataloging-in-Publication Data

Johnson, Melissa Ewey.
   Halle Berry : a biography / Melissa Ewey Johnson.
     p. cm. — (Greenwood biographies)
   Includes bibliographical references and index.
   Includes filmography.
   ISBN 978–0–313–35834–0 (hard copy : alk. paper) — ISBN 978–0–313–35835–7 (ebook) 1. Berry, Halle. 2. Motion picture actors and actresses—United States—Biography. 3. African American motion picture actors and actresses—Biography. I. Title. II. Series.
PN2287.B4377J76   2010
791.4302´8092—dc22   2009034126
[B]

14 13 12 11 10   1 2 3 4 5

This book is also available on the World Wide Web as an eBook.
Visit www.abc-clio.com for details.

ABC-CLIO, LLC
130 Cremona Drive, P.O. Box 1911
Santa Barbara, California 93116-1911

This book is printed on acid-free paper ∞

Manufactured in the United States of America

CONTENTS

Series Foreword   vii

Introduction   ix

Timeline: Events in the Life of Halle Berry   xiii

Chapter 1   Growing Up Different   1

Chapter 2   Emerging Beauty in the Professional Pageant World   13

Chapter 3   Breaking into the Big Time   25

Chapter 4   Tough Breaks   39

Chapter 5   Top of Her Game   55

Chapter 6   The Road to Fulfillment   83

Appendix A: Halle Berry Filmography and Television Appearances   105

Appendix B: Some of Halle Berry's Major Award Wins
         and Nominations   109

Further Reading   117

Index   119

Photo essay follows page 38

SERIES FOREWORD

In response to high school and public library needs, Greenwood developed this distinguished series of full-length biographies specifically for student use. Prepared by field experts and professionals, these engaging biographies are tailored for high school students who need challenging yet accessible biographies. Ideal for secondary school assignments, the length, format, and subject areas are designed to meet educators' requirements and students' interests.

Greenwood offers an extensive selection of biographies spanning all curriculum related subject areas including social studies, the sciences, literature and the arts, history and politics, as well as popular culture, covering public figures and famous personalities from all time periods and backgrounds, both historic and contemporary, who have made an impact on American and/or world culture. Greenwood biographies were chosen based on comprehensive feedback from librarians and educators. Consideration was given to both curriculum relevance and inherent interest. The result is an intriguing mix of the well known and the unexpected, the saints and sinners from long-ago history and contemporary pop culture. Readers will find a wide array of subject choices from fascinating crime figures like Al Capone to inspiring pioneers like Margaret Mead, from the greatest minds of our time like Stephen Hawking to the most amazing success stories of our day like J. K. Rowling.

While the emphasis is on fact, not glorification, the books are meant to be fun to read. Each volume provides in-depth information about the subject's life from birth through childhood, the teen years, and adulthood. A thorough account relates family background and education, traces personal and professional influences, and explores struggles, accomplishments, and contributions. A timeline highlights the most significant life events against a historical perspective. Bibliographies supplement the reference value of each volume.

INTRODUCTION

Gorgeous. Talented. Driven.

These are but a few of the words that have been used to describe Academy Award–winning actress and international icon of beauty Halle Berry.

Halle has always radiated natural loveliness, a devastating combination of a delicate bone structure, a curvaceous physique, luminous skin that appears to be lit from within, and a flawless, disarming smile. These attributes have made Halle a world-renowned sex symbol and a regular member of *People* magazine's 50 Most Beautiful lists. She is the subject of hundreds of fan Web sites and a regular part of the wall décor of teenage boys and college students everywhere.

And Halle Berry's talent is undeniable: from her first on-screen appearance as a crack addict in the gritty Spike Lee–directed drama *Jungle Fever* (1991) to her portrayal of a superhero in comic book–based cult classic *X-Men* (2000) and her stark, vulnerable performance as a grieving widow in *Things We Lost in the Fire* (2007), she commands the attention of the viewer and fills the screen with her dynamic presence. Halle has played both major and minor parts in ensemble films, urban romantic tales, slapstick comedies, biblical stories, biographies, action-adventures, suspenseful thrillers, and more—and to each role, she brings authenticity and emotion, the kind of real portrayals that actors and actresses spend years studying in an attempt to capture.

Halle's career in film and television is notable for many reasons, but one of the most significant is that many of the parts she has played were written with a White actress in mind. And while Halle is the product of a biracial and bicultural union (her mother is White and British, her father was African-American), her caramel-colored skin prevented many Hollywood decision makers even from considering her for many coveted roles.

But Halle Berry is nothing if not persistent. A handful of dream roles may have eluded her, but she was able to audition for and secure several parts based on her willingness to immerse herself in her characters and go the extra mile—even, on a handful of occasions, paying her own way to travel across the country to read for a role.

That same persistence led her to make two projects that may have otherwise passed her by. Ever since Halle was a little girl, she dreamed of one day playing Dorothy Dandridge, the legendary, Academy Award–nominated (for the 1954 dramatic musical *Carmen Jones*) African-American actress and international icon. Perhaps it was not just coincidence that Dandridge and Halle were born in the same hospital in Cleveland: when it seemed as though Halle was about to miss her chance to portray her idol, she bought a screenplay, successfully pitched the project to the cable network Home Box Office (HBO), and went on to executive-produce and star in the film *Introducing Dorothy Dandridge* (1999), a role that would earn Halle a Golden Globe, critical acclaim, and the respect of her Hollywood peers.

But it was a big part in a small, independent film that would earn Halle a significant place in cinematic history. Her raw, searing portrayal of a woman who hits rock-bottom and embarks on an unlikely romance in *Monster's Ball* (2001) earned her the Academy Award for Best Actress—making her the first African-American woman to take home the award for a leading role. In her emotional, tear-filled speech, Halle thanked all of the nameless, faceless women of color who had come before her and tried to make their Hollywood dreams come true. "This moment is so much bigger than me," she said. "Tonight, the doors have been opened."[1]

The Oscar put Halle on the top of the Hollywood feeding chain at last, but it seemed as though true happiness had eluded her. Halle had endured two failed marriages and several additional relationships filled with drama, but in 2008, at the age of 41, she would not only find contentment as the life partner of a male model named Gabriel Aubry, but she also fulfilled another of her lifelong dreams—that of giving birth to a child (daughter Nahla Ariela).

With her personal life finally in a good place, Halle has promised that the best is yet to come. Not bad for a woman who started life as a little colored girl in the Midwest who longed for a place to belong and imagined that some day she would see her name in lights—and made that dream come true beyond even her own wildest dreams.

NOTE

1. "Halle Berry Wins Best Actress Oscar for 'Monster's Ball,'" Agence France-Presse—English, March 25, 2002.

TIMELINE: EVENTS IN THE LIFE OF HALLE BERRY

1966   Born in Cleveland, Ohio, on August 14.
1970   Halle's father walks out on his wife and two young children.
1971   Judith Berry moves with her children to Oakwood Village, Ohio.
1984   Is named Prom Queen at Bedford High School.
        Graduates from Bedford High School.
1985   Wins the Miss Teen All American Pageant.
        Enrolls in journalism courses at Cuyahoga Community College in Ohio.
1986   Wins the Miss Ohio Pageant.
        Named first runner-up in the Miss USA Pageant.
        Drops out of Cuyahoga Community College.
        Places sixth in the Miss World Pageant.
1989   Cast in the TV sitcom *Living Dolls*.
        Collapses on the set of *Living Dolls* and spends a week in a coma.
        Is diagnosed with Type 1 diabetes.
1990   *Living Dolls* is canceled after 12 episodes.
1991   Appears in a guest role in the short-lived TV sitcom *They Came from Outer Space*.
        Appears in an episode of the college-based TV sitcom *A Different World*.

Appears in an episode of *Amen*, a TV sitcom that takes place in a church.

Takes the role of vixen Debbie Porter on the TV nighttime soap opera *Knots Landing*.

Is cast in her first film role, playing a crack addict in *Jungle Fever*.

Plays nightclub promoter Natalie in the romantic comedy *Strictly Business*.

Plays Cory, an exotic dancer, in *The Last Boy Scout*.

1992   Meets David Justice, baseball player for the Atlanta Braves.

Ends her run on *Knots Landing* after appearing in 21 episodes.

1993   Marries David Justice in a private ceremony in Atlanta on January 1.

Appears as Autumn Haley, a brainy college student in *The Program*.

Plays Kathleen Mercer, an investigative reporter, in *Father Hood*.

Plays the title role of *Queen* in the television miniseries based on a book by Alex Haley.

1994   Plays Rosetta Stone in a live-action film version of the cartoon classic *The Flintstones*.

Announces that she and husband David Justice are separating.

Is named one of *People* magazine's "50 Most Beautiful People" in May for the first time.

1995   Plays Khaila Richards, an addict trying to regain custody of her son, in *Losing Isaiah*.

Plays Queen Sheba in the TV movie *Solomon and Sheba*.

1996   Plays a flight attendant in the action flick *Executive Decision*.

Plays desperate woman Josie Potenza in *The Rich Man's Wife*.

Stars in the movie *Race the Sun* as Miss Sandra Beecher, a high school teacher.

Becomes a spokesmodel for Revlon cosmetics.

Files for divorce from David Justice.

1997   Plays a ghetto-fabulous diva named Nisi in the comedy *B.A.P.S.*

Divorce from David Justice is final, officially ending their marriage.

1998   Appears in the biography film *Why Do Fools Fall in Love?* as
        1950s singer Zola Taylor.
        Plays Nina, a streetwise woman who takes up with an aging
        politician, in *Bulworth*.
        Stars in the television movie *Oprah Winfrey Presents: The
        Wedding*, based on a classic novel by Harlem Renaissance
        writer Dorothy West.
        Hosts an episode of the sketch comedy television show
        Mad tv.

1999   Serves as executive producer and star of the HBO movie
        Introducing Dorothy Dandridge.
        Starts dating rhythm and blues singer Eric Benét.

2000   Allegedly causes a hit-and-run car accident and is sentenced
        to pay a fine and perform community service.
        Becomes engaged to Eric Benét.
        Plays Storm in *X-Men*, a film based on the popular Marvel
        Comics comic books.
        Wins an Emmy Award for Outstanding Lead Actress in a
        Miniseries for her portrayal of Dorothy Dandridge in *Intro-
        ducing Dorothy Dandridge*.

2001   Marries Eric Benét.
        Plays Ginger Knowles, a woman who works for a powerful
        criminal, in *Swordfish*.
        Plays Leticia Musgrove, the wife of a death-row convict, in
        the independent film *Monster's Ball*.

2002   Is announced on February 12 as an Academy Award
        nominee in the Best Actress category for *Monster's Ball*, only
        the second African-American woman to ever have been
        nominated.
        Wins the Academy Award for Best Actress on March 24 for
        her role in *Monster's Ball*, becoming the first African-
        American woman in history to win the award.
        Wins an Emmy Award for Outstanding Lead Actress—Mini-
        series or a Movie for *Introducing Dorothy Dandridge*.
        Wins the Golden Globe Award for Best Performance by an
        Actress in a Mini-Series or Motion Picture Made for Televi-
        sion for *Introducing Dorothy Dandridge*.

Stars in the James Bond movie *Die Another Day* as Jinx, an international spy and Bond's love interest.

Graces the December cover of *Vogue* magazine.

2003   Receives a dramatic kiss from actor Adrien Brody (*The Pianist*) after she presents him with the Best Actor Oscar at the 75th Academy Awards.

Reprises her role as Storm in *X-Men 2: X-Men United*.

Plays Miranda Grey, a psychiatrist who becomes a patient, in the horror thriller *Gothika*.

Estranged father Jerome Berry dies in a nursing home.

2004   Announces on April 27 that she has filed for divorce from husband Eric Benét.

Plays Patience Phillips and her superhero alter ego in "*Catwoman.*"

2005   Stars in the television movie *Their Eyes Were Watching God* as Janie Crawford, a free-spirited woman searching for happiness. The movie is based on the 1937 book of the same name by African-American female author Zora Neale Hurston.

Briefly dates actor Michael Ealy, her *Their Eyes Were Watching God* costar.

Appears in print ads and television commercials for Revlon, a cosmetics company.

Wins the Razzie Award for Worst Actress for her performance in *Catwoman*.

Becomes a spokesperson for Novo Nordisk, a pharmaceutical company that makes products for diabetics.

Voices the character Cappy in the animated movie *Robots*.

Appears in ads as a spokesmodel for Versace.

Meets model Gabriel Aubry and starts dating him.

2006   Reprises her role as cartoon superhero Storm in *X-Men: The Last Stand*, the final installment in the X-Men series.

Ranks number 65 on *Forbes* magazine's list of "The Top 100 Celebrities" for earning a reported $16 million.

2007   Plays Rowena Price, a journalist investigating the murder of her friend, in *Perfect Stranger*.

Portrays Audrey Burke, a woman recovering from the sudden death of her husband, in *Things We Lost in the Fire*.

Announces that she is pregnant; Gabriel Aubry is the father.

Endorses presidential candidate Barack Obama; contributes money and donates her time to his political campaign.

Appears on the Bravo television show *Inside The Actor's Studio* on October 29.

2008   Signs deal with Coty to launch a signature perfume line, "Halle by Halle Berry."

Gives birth on March 16 to a daughter, whom she and boyfriend Gabriel Aubry name Nahla Ariela.

2009   Launches a signature fragrance, Halle by Halle Berry.

Information for this chronology was taken from Internet Movie Database (imdb.com).

Chapter 1

GROWING UP DIFFERENT

Cleveland, Ohio, an American city on the coast of Lake Erie and home to the Rock and Roll Hall of Fame and Museum, may not seem at first glance to have been a glamorous destination that catered to the rich and famous. Indeed, the once-booming industrial mecca (coal and iron ore were the area's main natural resources) experienced a decline after World War II that continued during the 1960s, but a landmark to a fading era stubbornly remained in business—the elegant Halle Brothers Co. department store, commonly known as Halle's. Founded by siblings Samuel Horatio Halle and Salmon Portland Chase Halle in 1891, their main location was based in downtown Cleveland and turned into a chain with several locations in the suburbs. A destination for Cleveland's well-to-do citizens, Halle Brothers sold designer clothing, furs, makeup, accessories, and housewares. It was the place to see and be seen, where socialites and heiresses did their shopping and the less well-off dared to dream of a more luxurious life.

For Judith Ann Hawkins, the fashionable allure of Halle's was a lifetime away from her roots in the town of Liverpool, England, where she was born in 1939 to Nellie and Earl Hawkins. Judith left her working-class hometown when she was 10 years old and relocated with her family across the Atlantic to the suburban enclave of Elyria, Ohio. Judith grew up to become a nurse and worked at a psychiatric hospital for war veterans in Cleveland, where she met Jerome Jessie Berry, an African-American man from Pennsylvania who was three years her junior. A U.S. Air Force veteran, Berry worked at the hospital as a porter (a person who transports patients around the hospital) and was divorced with two children from his previous marriage—a daughter, Renee, and a son, Anthony.

Judith and Jerome dated one another and fell in love. When Judith became pregnant, they where quickly married—much to the displeasure of Judith's conservative and closed-minded parents. When they learned that their White daughter had married a Black man—a union that was considered taboo at the time by many people on both sides of the Atlantic Ocean—Judith's mother and father disowned her and never spoke to her again. Defiant, the couple settled into a home on East 177th Street in Cleveland in a predominantly Black neighborhood. They had two daughters: Heidi Berry, who was born in early 1966, and Maria Halle, born on August 14 later that same year. Judith gave her younger daughter the middle name of Halle in honor of the iconic department store she loved, which was starting to lose its former glory but still held a warm place in the young mother's memory. Halle made her debut into the world in the same hospital where Dorothy Dandridge—the iconic African-American actress who broke color barriers in the 1950s and 1960s and who Halle would later play to critical acclaim in a movie—was born on November 9, 1922.

In 1971, Maria Halle's name was legally changed to Halle Maria. It is unclear exactly why the name change took place, but one can imagine that her parents took to calling her Halle instead of Maria, and that the name Halle was more distinctive, even unique—a moniker that suited a child that would soon grow up to be anything but ordinary.

A TURBULENT TIME

The first few years of Halle Berry's life took place during a turbulent time in American history. The iconic rock and roll bands The Beatles (who hailed from Liverpool, the same English hometown as Halle's mother Judith Berry) and the Rolling Stones were at the top of the music charts, African-American athlete Muhammad Ali won the world heavyweight boxing title, and the number of American troops being sent to fight in the Vietnam War was at an all-time high. Lyndon B. Johnson was the president of the United States until he was succeeded by Richard M. Nixon, who would leave the White House in disgrace in August 1974 following the Watergate scandal.

The civil rights era, during which activists and protestors fought to change laws and attitudes that kept African-Americans from enjoying the same access to jobs, education, housing, and public spaces as Whites, had taken a beating with the recent assassinations of Martin Luther King, Jr., Malcolm X, and Bobby Kennedy; and political and social unrest were at an all-time high. Racial tensions had peaked in the United States, and urban areas were especially hard-hit by the one-two punch of economic declines and a growing sense of animosity between African-Americans and Whites. There were two major race riots in the city of Halle's birth in the 1960s: the Hough Riots the year she was born and the Glenville Shootout in 1968. Both of those incidents lasted for several days and resulted in a total of 11 deaths, hundreds of arrests, and massive destruction of public property.

Reflective of the growing racial animosity of the times was the continuing existence of laws that banned interracial marriages. Known formally in the legal systems as anti-miscegenation laws, they made such marriages illegal and threatened anyone who broke the laws with arrest and imprisonment. While those laws were rarely enforced, there was still a social stigma about marrying outside your race in the United States.

Interracial marriage was not a new thing in the 1960s, but public acknowledgment was rare and mainstream acceptance was almost unheard of. When Rat Packer (and African-American) entertainer Sammy Davis, Jr. married the blonde, Swedish movie startlet May Britt on November 13, 1960, the public at large was enraged and both were met with death threats and professional backlash. Blacks felt betrayed that their beloved star married outside his race.

The anti-miscegenation laws were still on the books in 16 states when, in 1967, the United States Supreme Court ruled in a landmark case, *Loving v. Virginia*, to repeal the remaining anti-miscegenation laws. The case involved a White man, Richard Loving, and a Black woman, Mildred, who married legally in Washington, D.C., but were jailed and forced to leave when they returned to their home in Caroline County, Virginia.[1]

For Halle, it was an especially difficult time to be a brown-skinned girl in the midwestern United States, particularly as the daughter of a

White mother and a Black father. Halle has always referred to Judith as her role model, but even as a child, she was aware of how different she looked from her mother. "My first memory as a kid was of my mother and her long blond hair—which she probably dyed," Halle once said. "It was just so different from mine. I remember looking at her and thinking how beautiful she was."[2]

Jerome Berry's family was less than accepting of his new White wife. Halle would later recall hearing some of her father's relatives refer to her mother as "the White bitch" and remembers moments when she and her sister were ostracized because they looked so much different from their father's side of the family.[3] Halle has never spoken publicly about any relationship she might have had with Renee and Anthony, the older half-siblings that her father had from a previous marriage.

Jerome, Judith, Heidi, and Halle stood out like a sore thumb in their Black inner-city Cleveland neighborhood, where the presence of White people was rare and the existence of a biracial family was practically unheard of. Halle and Heidi were both beautiful, friendly little girls, but their caramel-colored skin and curly hair made them distinctly different in appearance from their neighbors, many of whom had never seen anyone who looked the way they did and had certainly never seen a White woman married to a Black man before. The Berry girls became something of a novelty, and they endured taunts and teasing outside of their home.

"When we lived in the black neighborhood, we weren't liked because my mother was white," Halle explained. "To me, color was never an issue. It was only when the other kids started to say things like, 'What's wrong with your mom?' or, 'That's not really your mom,' that I started to think about it."[4]

There were no other mixed-race children around that Halle could relate to, and she felt torn between the cultures and identities that separated Black and White in the world she lived in. Why, Halle must have wondered, did other people make her feel as though she had to choose to be one or the other? Why could she not just identify as both? To help Halle come to terms with her confusing racial identity, her mother instructed her to call herself "Black" because when people looked at her, that is what they would think she was,[5] and let her know that she was not abandoning the White side of her family by doing so.[6]

Inside the Berry household, things were even more troublesome. Years later, Halle would recall how Jerome Berry's social drinking evolved into a swift and steady descent into alcoholism and substance abuse, with marijuana being his main drug of choice. Even more horrifying was the physical and mental abuse he directed toward Halle's mother and sister. Jerome and Judith's fights became more and more frequent, and when those arguments became physical, it was a young Heidi who tried to break them up. Halle told a reporter how Heidi would try to stand in between her parents to keep her father from hitting her mother, and she often found herself caught in the middle and became another outlet for Jerome's growing, unrelenting anger. Halle's memories of those turbulent times include an incident when her father threw the family puppy against a wall, but she never endured his rage and remembers feeling tremendous guilt that she was spared from her father's abuse while her mother and sister were not.[7,8]

When Halle was four years old, Jerome Berry abandoned his wife and daughters and moved out of their home, never once offering to provide monetary support or coming to visit his children during the several years that followed. Heartbroken but not defeated, Judith was relieved that she and her daughters were out of harm's way. Seeing his departure as an opportunity to regroup, Judith decided to give her girls a chance to lead more successful lives and put them on a path that would allow them to make their dreams come true. After driving past the high school where her daughters would eventually enroll and finding it run down and covered in graffiti,[9] Judith realized that their gritty neighborhood lacked the strong educational system that would give her girls a chance to excel and grow up to become confident, independent women. The young mother quickly packed up all of their worldly possessions and swiftly relocated 18 miles southeast of Cleveland to the predominately White suburb of Oakwood Village.

ESCAPE TO THE SUBURBS

The sleepy, tree-lined enclave of Oakwood Village, Ohio, made much of its diversified population and family-friendly vibe on its Web site in 2009 ("Welcome to Our Proud and Progressive Community," the home page proclaimed), but in 1970, when Judith moved there with her two mixed-race daughters who looked more Black than White, they were not exactly greeted by a welcome wagon full of progressive, racially tolerant neighbors. The local kids, just like the kids from the Berry's old neighborhood in Cleveland, took to calling Halle and Heidi mean and hurtful names. This time, the girls were frequently called "zebras," "half-breeds," and "Oreo cookies" (as in black on the outside, white on the inside) and were teased mercilessly for looking too exotic, too unusual, and too different from the standard blonde hair, blue eyes, and peaches-and-cream–complexioned ideal of all-American attractiveness.

However, thanks to Judith's strong parenting skills, Halle and Heidi learned to shrug off the taunts and became well-liked model students who earned top grades and quickly moved to the heads of their classes. "It was a little bit of a culture shock for me at first, leaving the environment of the inner city and going to the 'burbs,"[10] said Berry. "My sister and I were among maybe five black kids at school."[11]

The bliss the girls shared with their mother was short-lived when Judith, thinking the girls would benefit from having a father around, reconciled with her husband and allowed him to move back in with her and the girls in 1976. Unfortunately, Jerome was still drinking, and the abuse picked up right where it left off. "That was probably one of the worst years of my life," Halle would later recall.

> And probably because I loved him so much, I think, on some level and desperately wanted a father. But having him come back into our home and being very violent and being an alcoholic and sort of abusing my mother and my sister, but never me, I think I grew up with a lot of guilt because . . . why not me? Yes. And that—it was the worst—the worst year.[12]

Jerome Berry's violent behavior finally reached a point to which Judith could endure no more. Halle has never discussed the exact circumstances of her father's departure, but it is known that he left the family for good a year after he had reinserted himself into their lives. For the rest of her adolescence and well into her adulthood, Halle was estranged from her father and would struggle with the repercussions that longing for a father figure would have on her self-esteem and personal relationships. It would be years before Halle would hear from her father again.

THE AMBITIOUS OVERACHIEVER

For Halle, the absence of a father meant that she was the one who had to fill a void within her fractured family unit. "I was so close to my mother and felt so protective of her that, when my father left, all I wanted to do was to make her happy," Halle has said. "I wanted to do well in school. I didn't want to disappoint her. She made it easy for me to accept who I was and embrace my blackness."[13]

Judith Berry would later recount to a British newspaper how difficult it was raising two young daughters on her own, without the assistance of a husband or even extended family members. She described her experiences as a single mother as tough, especially where finances were concerned. Judith was not making a lot of money at her nursing job, and she recalled that there were often times when she could not afford to take Halle and Heidi to the movies. Judith did the best she could for her daughters and worked long hours to support them and provide money for the little extras, such as fashionable new clothes, so they would not feel out of place among their friends from households with two working parents or a father with a lucrative enough career to support a stay-at-home mother. Halle later recalled how her mother would wear the same pair of shoes for years, choosing to spend whatever spare money she had on Halle and her sister.

The lower middle-class Berry family was far from destitute, but from where Halle stood, it was hard to imagine a future in which her options were limited only by her imagination. Years later, Halle would recall how *The Wizard of Oz*, the classic 1939 film starring Judy Garland that she probably saw on television, allowed her to imagine a life that was vastly different from her reality. "It was the first time I saw a movie that allowed me to dream," she said. "I really couldn't see outside of the boundaries of my own backyard either. And with this movie, I got to travel to this magical place."[14]

Despite the hope that watching *The Wizard of Oz* gave her, Halle struggled with self-doubt throughout her adolescence and was in danger of falling into a dark and dangerous emotional void. The lack of African-American faces to look up to on a regular basis confused Halle, who remembered coming home from school with her sister in the afternoon to watch such shows as *General Hospital* and reruns of *The Little Rascals* on television and being dismayed at the lack of

characters that looked like she and her sister did—or, in the case of the
Rascals, irritated at the buffoonery of Buckwheat, who seemed to Halle
and much of Black America to be a cruel stereotype of their race.[15]

The years of her father's abuse had taken a toll on young Halle's
emotional well-being, and her mother put her in therapy starting at the
age of 10 to help her deal with her issues.[16] Professional help aside, Halle
was in desperate need of a friend and mentor. Luckily, when Halle
entered the fifth grade, she met Yvonne Sims, a woman who would
become an influential role model. Sims was the only African-American
teacher in Halle's school, and she and Halle developed an instant bond.
Halle credits Sims with saving her from possibly veering down a path
lined with bad choices and lowered expectations. "She took me in and
loved me," Halle recalled, "and through her I knew that I was okay and
smart and talented. She will always be someone I admire."[17]

Thanks to the influence of Sims and her mother, Halle attempted to
cope with her difficult past and tried to live the life of a normal teenager: she hung out at nearby Randall Park Mall with her friends, went
out on dates (Halle has recounted many times that her chest developed
faster than other girls her age, which undoubtedly improved her
popularity with the boys), and liked going to the movies and listening
to pop music. She had developed from a cute, precocious young girl
into a stunning young woman, with her caramel-colored skin, dark,
beguiling eyes, and a dazzling smile.

But Halle was not content to rely on her good looks to get ahead.
In spite of her physical appeal and growing popularity, Halle still felt
alienated and alone; her desire to be accepted by her peers drove her
to be the best at everything, pushing her to get top grades in her classes
and become very involved in extracurricular activities. She attended
Heskett Middle School and Bedford High School, where, in an attempt
to stand out as one of the only Black faces in a sea of 1,500 students,
she became a member of the academic honor society, fashion editor
of the school paper, and class president. She was also the head cheer-
leader for the school sports teams, the Bearcats.

TEENAGE BEAUTY QUEEN

Halle also dabbled in acting and participated in several school drama
projects, including a memorable turn her senior year as Tillie, the

leading role in a production of the dramatic, Pulitzer Prize–winning play *The Effect of Gamma Rays on Man-in-the-Moon Marigolds* by Paul Zindel. The play is a Tennessee Williams–style tale of a dysfunctional family headed by an abusive single mother. Halle played one of the daughters, who prepares for a science fair project in spite of her mother's jealous attempts to sabotage her efforts. This may have been an early hint of what the future had in store for Halle, but her focus shifted in 1983 when Gregory Lewis, a young man who was reportedly Halle's first serious high school boyfriend,[18] secretly sent two pictures of Halle to the Miss Teen Ohio beauty pageant committee. Attracted by the chance to win money that she could put toward paying for college, Halle went on to compete and won the title.

Meanwhile, Halle's name was added to the short list of girls at Bedford High School who were nominated for senior prom queen. Halle received the majority of the votes, but her joy was short-lived when some of her classmates accused her of stuffing the ballot box and tried to take her crown away. Dennis Blackburn, the school principal, recalled that the vote was a tie. "If she was accused of stuffing the ballot box, it was not by any adult," he later said.[19]

After the matter was investigated, Halle was not found to be at fault, but it was decided that, in the interest of "fairness," the girls would share the title of prom queen. "I had worked so hard to be accepted, but when it came to being a standard of beauty for the school, they didn't want me,"[20] Halle later recalled. "They couldn't deny me my grade point average or my ability to edit a newspaper, but when it came to beauty, it was a problem."[21]

Halle accepted the decision to share the crown, but the other girl refused to do so and fought to have the right to have the prom queen title all to herself. The final decision came down to a coin toss in the assistant principal's office—and fate flipped the coin in Halle's favor.

Victorious but still hurt by the allegations of cheating, Halle attempted to shake off the controversy and prepare for the big day. In the weeks leading up to the prom, she was amused to discover that someone was leaving chocolate and cream cookies in her family's mailbox. Halle thought they were from an admirer until she told her friends about it. She was crushed to learn that the cookies were a joke—a mean-spirited reference to her mixed-race heritage.

The night before the prom there was a celebratory dinner held for members of the prom court, and the prom queen was to have a seat of honor at the front of the room. Halle was still so upset about the accusations of cheating to win that she almost did not attend. Her mother convinced her that if she did not show up, it would mean that she had let her detractors win, so Halle put on a brave face and waltzed into the dinner a half hour before it was over. Halle has since acknowledged that it took her a long time to get over the slight.

In retrospect, the prom queen incident provided important life lessons that Halle would draw from throughout the rest of her life: that things were not always going to be fair; that no matter how nice she was, people would try to rain on her parade and say things that were not true; that she would have to fight to get the opportunities and recognition that she deserved; and that sometimes, it truly is lonely at the top.

The crowns Halle Berry earned as prom queen and as Miss Teen Ohio may have weighed heavy on her head at times, but those experiences were about to open a whole new world of possibilities for the brainy teenage beauty—a world that would take her beyond the limited opportunities of life in the Midwest and put her in a position to achieve fame and wealth on an international stage.

NOTES

1. "Loving Decision: 40 Years of Legal Interracial Unions," National Public Radio, http://www.npr.org/templates/story/story.php?storyId=10889047.

2. "Halle Berry on Motherhood," *cnn.com*, http://www.cnn.com/2008/LIVING/homestyle/01/14/halle.berry/index.html#cnnSTCText.

3. "Halle Berry on Overcoming Racism," *Sunday Mirror* (London), July 1, 2001.

4. Barbara Davies, "A Star against All Odds," *Daily Mail* (London), May 19, 2007.

5. "Berry Happy at Last," *Daily Mirror* (London), April 16, 2007.

6. Davies, "A Star against All Odds."

7. "Profile of Halle Berry," CNN, November 28, 2002.

8. Davies, "A Star against All Odds."

9. "Halle Berry Interview: Closer to Home," http://www.rd.com/celebrities/halle-berry-closer-to-home/article35264-1.html.

10. Clint O'Connor, "Halle Berry on Home, Work and the Public Glare," *Cleveland Plain Dealer Extra*, April 5, 2007.

11. Diane Weathers, "Halle Berry Interview: Closer to Home," *Reader's Digest*, August 2007.

12. CNN Interview, *Larry King Live*.

13. Davies, "A Star against All Odds."

14. AFI's (American Film Institute) 100 Years, 100 Movies—10th Anniversary Edition.

15. "Throwing Stones," *Toronto Sun*, May 30, 1994.

16. "The Bond Girl Who Has Been in Therapy," *Evening Standard* (London), November 20, 2002.

17. Weathers, "Halle Berry Interview: Closer to Home."

18. Siobhan Synnot, "Halle's Blazing Comet," *Scotland on Sunday* (Edinburgh), November 21, 2002.

19. "Beyond Face Value," *Mail on Sunday* (London), May 7, 1995.

20. Jill Gerston, "The Prom's Co-Queen Finally Gets Her Revenge," *New York Times*, March 12, 1995.

21. "Beyond Face Value."

Chapter 2

EMERGING BEAUTY IN THE PROFESSIONAL PAGEANT WORLD

In the 1980s, the standards that defined American beauty—the blonde-haired, blue-eyed, corn-fed ideal—were evolving to reflect both the country's increasingly diverse population and the growing acknowledgment that the definitions of attractiveness could no longer be limited to one race. Mainstream magazines, such as *Vogue*, *Cosmopolitan*, and *Madamoiselle* were putting Black models on their covers (Iman and Beverly Johnson were two of the top Black models of the decade) on a regular basis, *The Cosby Show* (starring beloved comedian Bill Cosby as a successful doctor and loving father) was a top-rated television sitcom, and the cable music network MTV (Music Television) was embracing the work of Black singers and musicians with monumental crossover appeal, such as pop superstars Lionel Ritchie, Tina Turner, Michael Jackson, and Prince.

The concept of beauty pageants has been around since ancient times, but the first modern pageant did not take place in the United States until the 1800s, when circus promoter P. T. Barnum staged competitions to draw attention to his traveling shows. In the decades that followed, "Bathing Beauty" contests were regularly held during summer festivals in resort towns and beach communities along the coasts of the nation.

The grandmother of all beauty pageants, the Miss America Pageant, started in Atlantic City, New Jersey, in 1921. It became a celebrated annual event and, when the contestants began to visit troops during

World War II, gained an image of respectability and prestige. Through the changing times, the Miss America Pageant evolved as women achieved equal rights and sought higher education—talent competitions and scholarships became the norm.

However, minorities were conspicuously absent from beauty pageants. The Miss America Pageant, in particular, barred Black contestants from entering the competition for decades. It was not until 1965 that Black contestant Sarah Peer, the African-American winner of the Miss Rochester Pageant, had a shot at winning the Miss America crown.

In 1970, the Miss Black Sacramento Pageant was created by Velma Stokley-Flournoy to give Black women the chance to compete in a pageant of their own. More ethnic pageants followed, including Miss Black America, Miss Latina, and Miss Asian America.[1]

Beauty pageants were big business during the early to mid 1980s, drawing crowds of adoring fans and scoring huge ratings when aired during prime-time television. Hometown crowds put a lot of support behind their local girls who competed in state, national, and international pageants, and the claiming of the crown was not only a source of civic pride but also provided a lucrative payoff (in the form of scholarships, cars, jewelry, and other sponsor-provided trinkets) for the winners. Gambling oddsmakers in Las Vegas and throughout the world even got in on the action, handicapping the contestants and taking bets on who would be the winner and where each girl would place in the final results.

Like the rest of society, beauty pageants were starting to take notice of beautiful, talented women of a variety of races and skin tones. Vanessa Williams—the pop singer and actress perhaps best known for her role on the ABC television sitcom *Ugly Betty*—made history in 1984 when she became the first African-American woman to win the Miss America Pageant. (Williams was forced to relinquish her crown 10 months later after a nude photo scandal, and her title officially went to the first runner-up, Suzette Charles, who was also Black.) It seemed that the doors had finally been flung open wide for other non-Caucasian women to reach for first place and bask in the rewards and recognition that a pageant title could provide. For little African-American girls, it was now possible to dream that they, too, could be pretty and talented enough to compete with their White counterparts and actually win top honors when they grew up.

PROFESSIONAL PAGEANT CONTESTANT

After Halle Berry graduated with top honors from Bedford High School in 1984, she realized that the attention and prizes she had received from her Miss Teen Ohio win were only the beginning of what her looks, charm, and talents could accomplish. Her title had brought with it a certain amount of local celebrity, giving the teenager a taste of what it felt like to be famous and appreciated as she traveled around her home state making public appearances wearing her crown and sash. There is little doubt that the experience may have inspired Halle to seek notoriety and opportunity on a much larger scale. With the ink on her new high school diploma barely dry, Halle decided to devote a significant amount of her time and energy to competing on the national beauty pageant circuit.

In 1985, Halle went on to represent Ohio in the Miss Teen All American Pageant. She won, becoming he first African-American in history to take the title. One year later, Halle won the Miss Ohio Pageant and became the first runner-up in the Miss USA Pageant. That same year, the then 20-year-old capitalized on the momentum and went to London, England, to compete in the Miss World Pageant.

Her participation courted a bit of controversy at a Variety Club luncheon that featured the contestants showing off their national costumes. Miss Holland wore a traditional dress and clogs, Miss India wore a conservative sari, but Halle showed up wearing a flesh-colored body stocking topped by a patriotic red, white, and blue bikini, complete with shooting stars and strings of beads. Halle claimed that the bikini, a creation of American designer Dick Frank, was meant to symbolize America's progress in space exploration and that she had only worn what she had been asked to wear by U.S. pageant officials. Some of the more conservative pageant judges and contestants were shocked, calling the outfit the skimpiest in the pageant's history and crying foul that Halle would undoubtedly have an unfair advantage by attracting publicity for her sexy attire.

While it may be debatable how much influence that revealing ensemble had on the Miss World judges (it certainly caught the attention of the international media and may have encouraged some of the 500 million viewers worldwide who watched the television broadcast of the pageant to tune in), one thing is certain: Halle was a formidable opponent, and her beauty, talent, and charm made her the first African-American to compete in the Miss World finals on November 14. "It makes me very proud to be the first," Halle said. "I hope other black women around the world, and especially in the United States, will look at me and use me as either a role model or just to show them that it can be done."[2]

Although Halle got to try on the crown, sash, and sceptre (an ornamental staff carried by royalty) during rehearsals and placed first in the interview portion of the competition, she would lose to Miss Trinidad and Tobago and place sixth overall. History-making wins and high placements aside, Halle credits her pageant experience with teaching her to appreciate the true power of her beauty and realize that her early pageant wins were not just a fluke. "I really believe in being a woman," Halle explained,

> and if you're blessed with certain attributes, I learned through beauty pageants and just being a woman that all those things can help you and you should use them to your advantage when you can. Not exploiting yourself, but that's definitely what makes a woman a woman and a man a man. I don't have a problem with showing that.[3]

MAKING THE TRANSITION

Halle was starting to dream of a career on the big screen and her name in huge letters on movie theater marquees, but at her mother's urgings, she decided to give formal education a try in an attempt to be more practical and have something to fall back on. Halle envisioned herself as an anchorwoman—something not unlike the Black equivalent of Barbara Walters and the other female news superstars of the day—and enrolled in broadcast journalism classes (with a minor in theater) at Cuyahoga Community College in Cleveland. However, she felt her attention wandering as the bright lights of the big cities of New York and Los Angeles beckoned her to pursue her true calling. After an internship at a television station revealed that she thought that asking people questions as a reporter felt too intrusive,[4] she abandoned her idea of a having a future career as a news reporter and dropped out of community college after only one semester. "I realized it wasn't the place for me," she would say later.[5]

Choosing to wholeheartedly devote her time to establishing a career in entertainment, Halle decided to try and break into the business through the world of professional modeling. In the late 1980s, most of the faces gracing advertisements and fashion photo shoots were White. Modeling had become a big business, and the top faces of the day were known as "supermodels" and became celebrities who could make millions of dollars from a single contract, selling everything from cosmetics and clothing to soft drinks and car tires. The top working models of the day were Christie Brinkley, Elle MacPherson, Carol Alt, and Cindy Crawford. African-American models such as Iman, Beverly Johnson, and Naomi Campbell were beginning to make inroads (Johnson, for example, was the first Black model to appear on the cover of *Vogue* in the 1970s, but that proved to be a rare occurrence). The fashion industry in New York would use random Black and other "exotic"-looking models on occasion as a novelty, but in the Midwest—home to dozens of companies that catered to mainstream ideals—it was difficult for a Black model to find the kind of steady work that would make a second job unnecessary.

Modeling was one way that several actresses—Isabella Rossellini, Christie Brinkley, and Paulina Porizkova found box-office success and critical acclaim for their roles in major motion pictures—transitioned into Hollywood. Halle had such tremendous success winning pageants in which she had been constantly praised for her natural beauty. While Halle's physical attractiveness was undeniable, however, there were two unchangeable things that would prevent her from attaining super-model status—her height and her race. To even be considered for most commercial or runway modeling jobs, a female model should be at least 5 feet, 10 inches tall—and Halle Berry stood at 5 feet, 7 inches tall in her bare feet. She quickly learned that most modeling agencies would not even consider her once they learned she was several inches shy of the industry standard. (British supermodel Kate Moss, who is the same height as Halle, would find success in the 1990s, but is still considered an exception to the minimum height rule.)

With glossy photos from her pageant days in hand, Halle called upon several of the top modeling agencies in New York City and went to open calls—predetermined days on which unsolicited women who want to be models show up at agencies for evaluations and possible representation—but she was turned away and was told that she would never make it as a model in Manhattan, Paris, Milan, or any of the other fashion capitals of the world. Crushed but persistent, Halle finally found representation with Legends Modeling Agency, a fledgling modeling agency founded in 1981 by Kay Mitchell that would become a force in the agency business and would later change its name to IMG Models. Mitchell had served as a judge in three of the beauty pageants that Halle had competed in and remembered her well. Mitchell recalled that when she met Halle, she thought she was "was short but photogenic," but was willing to overlook her lack of height and give the retired beauty queen a shot as a professional model. Mitchell also sympathized with Halle's fall from grace: "Everybody's waving at you, and the next day you're nobody again,"[6] she said of Halle's rough transition from pageants to professional modeling.

The Legends Modeling Agency was based in New York City but had an office in Chicago, where models were often booked to do commercial and catalog work—not the high-fashion runway and magazine editorial gigs that Halle wanted to do. However, models that regularly booked commercial jobs could easily make six-figure salaries, so Halle decided to pack her bags and relocate to the Windy City.

Halle's mother, Judith, put Halle and several suitcases packed with all of Halle's worldly possessions into the family minivan and drove her seven hours from Ohio to her destination on the Illinois lakefront. It was an emotional journey—Judith was visibly upset that her 21-year-old daughter was striking out on her own and moving so far away from home. "She cried her eyes out all the way," Halle recalled. "I never came back."[7]

That move also marked the end of what had become a contentious relationship with her older sister, Heidi. Their dynamic had been filled with ups and downs during their adolescent years, and years later, Halle admitted that they fought often—not just verbal arguments, but physical fights in which blood was drawn. Their fragile relationship became even more distant when Halle left Heidi and Ohio behind to start her new life, and the two sisters reportedly have not spoken since and continue to be estranged from one another.[8] Indeed, photos of Heidi have never surfaced in the media, and she has never granted a single interview. Heidi is reportedly married with three children and lives in England, the birth country of her mother.

Contrary to popular belief, Halle's sister Heidi is not a singer—that is another woman, born in Boston who coincidentally also relocated to England, who shares the same name and recorded several albums in the 1990s.[9]

SURVIVING ON HER OWN

Halle settled in to her life in Chicago as an independent woman, going on several "go-sees" (the modeling equivalent of auditioning for jobs with potential clients) in her daily efforts to find work. She was able to book random assignments doing print advertisements and posing for clothing catalogs—at some photo shoots, she had to stand on stacks of telephone books to look as tall as the other models—but Halle had to take on a roommate to make ends meet. A few weeks after making her big move to Chicago, Halle booked a job in Milwaukee, Wisconsin, a city 90 miles to the north. When she returned from the job to her shared apartment, Halle was stunned to discover that her roommate had packed up and left—and stiffed Halle on her share of unpaid rent. Halle was not making enough money to establish a savings account and was basically living paycheck-to-paycheck, so there was no money leftover to take care of any emergencies.

Unable to pay the $1,200 tab on her own and facing the possibility of eviction, Halle called the one person in her life she could always count on: her mother. But to Halle's surprise, Judith was unsympathetic to her daughter's plea for assistance. "You wanted to go there," Judith told Halle during a tense, tearful phone call. "Now you're seeing what it's like in the real world."[10] Halle was so angry with her mother that she stopped calling her, and a year would pass before the mother and daughter would reconcile and bury the hatchet.

Desperate to make ends meet and pay off her debt, Halle cut corners and reduced her expenses any way she could—showing up at happy hour at local bars for the free buffalo wings or going hungry for days at a time.[11] Halle was on her own and all alone, with no one to loan her money or take her in. It was one of the toughest periods in Halle's life, and she nearly gave up on her dreams of stardom. She admits that if she had not been so scared during this time, she might have attempted suicide. But Halle persevered, vowing that she would do whatever it took to survive:

> It taught me how to take care of myself and that I could live through any situation, even if it meant going to a shelter for a small stint, or living within my means, which were meager. I became a person who knows that I will always make my own way.[12]

It was sometime after this dark period that Halle became involved with John Ronan, a Chicago-based dentist that she met through a friend of a friend. The two dated from 1989 to 1991, and Rowan assisted the struggling model and actress financially throughout their relationship. In an interview with *JET* magazine, Ronan said, "I told her, 'If you really want to be an actress, I'll help you' . . . I committed to her financially for three years, regardless of what happened to our relationship."[13]

CATCHING A BREAK ON THE SMALL SCREEN

Over time, Halle began booking regular work as a lingerie and catalog model. In between modeling jobs, Halle was taking acting classes at The Second City Training Center, the famed Chicago acting school that counts comedians Mike Myers, Tina Fey, and Stephen Colbert among its alumni. While she worked to hone her acting skills, Halle went out on numerous auditions, including several for daytime soap operas. She sent tapes of her monologues to casting agents; in 1989 she received a call from Vincent Cirrincione, a talent manager based in New York City. He offered to represent Halle if she would move to New York, give up modeling, and focus on her acting full time. Halle leapt at the opportunity, even though her finances were once again so tight that she stayed in a homeless shelter for a few days before friends got her a room in safer, but only slightly better, accommodations at a Manhattan YMCA.

Halle started going out on several auditions a day with headshots in hand and hope in her heart. It was not long before she landed a plum role on a promising new sitcom—in a case of art imitating life, the show was about young women trying to make it in the high-fashion modeling industry.

Living Dolls was a spin-off of the hit ABC network sitcom *Who's the Boss?*, which starred actors Tony Danza, Judith Light, and Alyssa Milano. The show's main character, a tough-but-pretty teenager named Charlie Briscoe (played by Leah Remini—years before she found fame on the popular CBS sitcom *The King of Queens*), was a friend of Milano's character, Samantha. Charlie tags along when Sam attempts to start a modeling career, and Charlie is the one chosen for representation by a teen-focused agency and sent to live in a house with her agent, her agent's son, and three other new models.

The *Living Dolls* characters were originally introduced on an episode of *Who's the Boss?*. Actress Vivica A. Fox (*Independence Day*, 1996, and *Kill Bill*, 2003) had originally been cast in the role of Emily Franklin, the beautiful, brainy girl with a special aptitude for science who was torn between the glamorous world of modeling and the more practical pursuit of a college degree and medical school. A pilot was shot and aired that used the same actors, but the network executives decided that the cast was not appealing enough and held new auditions to fill most of the roles. When the show was reshot to air during the beginning of the fall television season in 1989, it was Halle Berry who was playing the part of Emily.

Halle moved from New York to California to tape the show at the Warner Bros. Studio Facilities in Burbank. *Living Dolls* premiered on September 26, 1989, on ABC. From the start, the show was panned by the critics and received negative reviews in the press (the magazine *Entertainment Weekly* gave it an "F," and the *Washington Times* called it a "sugar-coated new pin-up show for teens"[14]), but Halle was so thrilled to have a role on national television that she ignored the negative reviews. In her eyes, she had finally made it, and she was the toast of Cleveland, Ohio, a local girl with a starring role on a well-publicized, major network television show.

Halle was working hard to keep up with the show's grueling production schedule and noticed one day that she felt more tired than usual. She had attributed her lack of energy to her demanding schedule and tried to press on and do her job, but she suddenly felt ill and passed out on the set.

Halle was rushed to the hospital, where doctors determined that she had type 1 diabetes. Previously called insulin-dependent diabetes mellitus or juvenile-onset diabetes, type 1 diabetes is a disease in which the body fails to produce or properly use insulin, the hormone that converts sugar, starches, and other food into energy. The cause of diabetes continues to be a mystery, although both genetics and environmental factors such as obesity and lack of exercise appear to play roles. Type 1 diabetes accounts for up to 10 percent of all diagnosed cases of diabetes and is most commonly diagnosed among children and young adults, but anyone can be diagnosed at any time.

Halle had fallen into a diabetic coma and did not wake up until a week later. A horrified Halle was told by her doctors that she would need to test her blood sugar levels on a daily basis, take insulin (either through injection via needles or an insulin pump), and carefully monitor her diet for the rest of her life—and if she did not, she would risk developing serious diabetic complications, such as blindness, heart disease, kidney failure, stroke, and possible amputations of her toes, feet, and other body parts.[15]

Halle was shocked to hear that she had a lifelong, potentially fatal health condition. At the age of 24, she did not know of anyone in her family who had type 1 diabetes and thought that her occasional bouts of exhaustion were a natural by-product of her hard work, not a symptom of a serious medical condition. Halle considers her coma to have been the wake-up call that forced her to take better care of herself. She made an effort to be more mindful of her stress levels, which could affect her blood sugar levels, and also took steps toward eating regular meals that are well-balanced nutritionally and low in sugar, fat, and processed carbohydrates. Exercise, something that she had done only sporadically, now became a part of her newfound healthy lifestyle. She would join a gym and eventually embrace yoga.

While Halle's health slowly recovered, her career experienced a big setback when Living Dolls tanked in the television ratings. Even though it initially aired after the highly successful situation comedy Who's the Boss? and moved to a prime Saturday night time slot following another popular half-hour show, Mr. Belvedere, Living Dolls failed to find an audience and was branded a flop. The show was canceled in December 1989 after only 13 episodes were aired. Despite knowing that dozens of television shows fail every year and that their demise does not always mean that the careers of their stars are over, Halle was distraught. She felt she had failed as an actress as she went without work for six long months.

Halle's personal life at this time was just as tumultuous as her professional life: According to Halle, in 1990, while on a trip to visit her mother back home in Cleveland, her on-again, off-again boyfriend from Chicago, John Ronan, allegedly let himself into her apartment and took back jewelry that he had given her as gifts—a ring and two gold necklaces—and stole a personal diary that Halle had been writing in regularly since 1985. Ronan denied all of the charges, and the diary never resurfaced.[16] In 1993, Ronan sued Halle for $80,000, claiming that he lent the actress money to help launch her career and that she never paid him back.[17]

Meanwhile, Halle continued to audition relentlessly, flying back and forth from Los Angeles to New York and sleeping on her manager's couch to save money. Halle was determined to succeed, but her résumé had more references to her pageant wins and modeling stints than her acting roles and was failing to catch the attention of casting agents. The young actress was still fighting an uphill battle to be taken seriously, and she was not content to audition for guest spots on random soap operas and sitcoms.

Halle still had her sights on big-screen box-office success, and even though many casting directors continued to see her as just another pretty face in a crowd of thousands of other pretty faces, she would have to go to extreme lengths to get a breakthrough role in a film by an up-and-coming maverick director that would get her noticed by some of Hollywood's top movers and shakers.

Notes

1. "Miss Sacramento Bee Sparks Delights—and Some Doubts," *Sacramento Bee*, May 3, 2009, http://www.sacbee.com/ourregion/story/1829529.html.

2. "First Black American Competes for Miss World Crown," Associated Press, November 12, 1986.

3. "Halle Berry Is on a Roll," BPI Entertainment News Wire, December 5, 1991.

4. "Meet Halle Berry," Knight Ridder/Tribune News Service, July 13, 2000.

5. "Berry Ripe for Action," *Courier Mail* (Brisbane, Queensland, Australia), May 2, 1996.

6. "Beyond Face Value," *Mail on Sunday* (London), May 7, 1995.

7. Ibid.

8. http://www.tcm.com/tcmdb/participant.jsp?spid=15188&apid=175874.

9. http://www.heidiberry.com/.

10. "Beyond Face Value."

11. "Halle Berry Once Lived in a Homeless Shelter!," *Hindustan Times*, March 15, 2007.

12. Ibid.

13. "Actress Halle Berry Hit with $80,000 Lawsuit by Chicago Dentist," *JET*, December 13, 1993.

14. Rick Marin, "Paper-Thin 'Dolls' Cut to Tease," *Washington Times*, September 26, 1989.

15. "Halle Berry: My Battle with Diabetes," *Daily Mail* (London), December 14, 2005.

16. "Beyond Face Value."

17. "Actress Halle Berry Hit with $80,000 Lawsuit by Chicago Dentist."

Chapter 3

BREAKING INTO THE BIG TIME

As the 1980s turned into the 1990s, Halle was still struggling to find success as an actress. The model-turned-actress label was following her everywhere, and it probably did not help her image that her biggest role to date had been playing a model on a critically panned sitcom. Despite the successful transitions a handful of models had in Hollywood, most had a role or two and quickly faded into obscurity. And those were cover girls with fame and recognizable names: Halle's modeling experience had been small-time in comparison, and no one in the entertainment industry knew her name. Instead of gaining recognition after *Living Dolls*, it was starting to seem that she would have to work harder than ever to prove that she was not just a pretty flash in the pan.

Halle managed to get bit parts and guest appearances on two popular, long-running sitcoms with predominately African-American casts that aired in early 1991—*Amen* (1986–1991), starring former *The Jeffersons* (1975–1985) star Sherman Hemsley as the pastor of a church; and *A Different World* (1987–1993), the spin-off of *The Cosby Show* (1984–1992) that was set at a historically black college. Halle also had a role on one episode of *They Came from Outer Space* (1990–1991), a sophomoric, forgettable situation comedy that centered on aliens sent to Earth to study humans and pick up women. *They Came from Outer Space* was canceled after 19 episodes.

However, 1991 would prove to be the year that Halle's perseverance would finally start to pay off in a major way. She would later recall that pivotal year as a whirlwind, one in which her acting career took off at a breakneck pace.

SOAP OPERA VIXEN

The early 1990s marked the peak of nighttime soap operas: one-hour long television serials that aired during prime time (generally the hours between 7 p.m. and 10 p.m.) and followed the love lives, business dealings, and complicated family dynamics of a select group of characters. Shows such as *Dallas* (1978–1991), *Dynasty* (1981–1989), and *Falcon Crest* (1981–1990) were pulling in millions of viewers every week who actively discussed the previous night's episodes around the water coolers at work. Even though the daytime soaps pulled respectable audiences, nighttime soaps reached millions of viewers who did not, or could not, follow the morning shows. As a result, nighttime soap stars were more well-known than their peers who toiled away during the daytime versions that were designed to entertain stay-at-home moms and retirees. The nighttime soaps were also much saucier, sexier, and more dramatic, and some cast members went on to have successful movie careers and gain international fame. The soaps were often a launching pad toward bigger and better parts, and many Hollywood A-listers paid their dues acting in one or two early in their professional careers.

In 1991, Halle landed a recurring role on nighttime soap opera *Knots Landing* (1979–1993), a spin-off of *Dallas* that was based in a wealthy seaside neighborhood in California and followed the complicated—and often downright scandalous—lives of Gary and Valene Ewing (relatives of *Dallas'* famed Ewing family) and their neighbors. *Knots Landing* would become the second longest-running drama to ever air on primetime network television, lasting for 14 seasons.

Halle successfully auditioned for the role of Debbie Porter, a young, saucy temptress who becomes the love interest of the character Frank Williams (played by actor Larry Riley) after his wife passes away. Debbie asks Frank out, but he initially turns her down because he thinks he is too old for her. Debbie persists, and a May-December romance develops; Debbie, however, breaks things off with Frank when she realizes that he is not ready for a serious relationship. Halle would perform the role for 21 episodes, from 1991 to 1992. After 14 seasons, *Knots Landing* would go off the air a year later.

Knots Landing gave Halle exposure on a whole new level—people were starting to recognize her on the streets, and casting directors who previously would not have given her the time of day were returning her calls and asking her to come in to read for roles. Random scripts were finally starting to be sent her way, but they were not the kind of movies that Halle wanted to be in. She was not satisfied to play the type of roles she was being offered—all of which were some sort of variation on the stereotypical "pretty girl":

> Those were the kind of parts that were coming my way, and I realized that unless that's how I wanted to spend my career, I'd have to shake them up a little bit and show I wasn't just relying on my physical self, but that I was willing to do character work. And dig deeper.[1]

BIG-SCREEN DREAMS BECOME A REALITY

The year 1991 was also when Halle's first movie role debuted. Spike Lee, an African-American director, had received accolades for his independent films, *She's Gotta Have It* (1986), *School Daze* (1988), *Do the Right Thing* (1989), and *Mo' Better Blues* (1990), and was casting roles for his next film.

Spike Lee has had a history of breaking the careers of dozens of actors, mainly by giving them an opportunity to act in roles created just for them. In *School Daze*, for example, was one of the first film roles that actor Samuel L. Jackson had ever had (Jackson played a local resident in a college town who gets into an argument with a group of students). Jackson went on to have a distinguished career in film (appearing in *Good Fellas*, 1990, *Jurassic Park*, 1993, and *Snakes on a Plane*, 2006). Another actor who broke out in a Lee film was Lawrence Fishburne (*The Matrix*, 1999), who had been stuck in dead-end television gigs (including a reoccurring role on the kids' show *Pee-Wee's Playhouse*) before his career got a jump start with his leading role in *School Daze*. Other actors whose careers benefited from roles in Lee's films include John Turturro, Michael Imperioli, Martin Lawrence, Denzel Washington, Wesley Snipes, and Mekhi Pfeiffer.

Jungle Fever (1991) tells the tale of an unlikely interracial romance between a married Black architect and a single Italian-American temporary secretary, and the impact their affair has on their families and on racial tensions in their neighborhoods. Wesley Snipes was cast as the architect, Flipper Purify, and Annabella Sciorra would play the part of Angie Tucci, his secretary and lover.

Spike Lee often cast himself in his own movies: in *Jungle Fever*, he took on the role of Cyrus, Flipper's best friend. Lee was looking for someone to play the role of his character's wife, Vera, and Halle Berry came in to audition for the part. Lee eventually decided that another model-turned-actress, Veronica Webb, was a better choice for the role, but told Halle that she could audition for another part in the script. Her choice surprised Lee: Halle told him that she wanted to try out for the smaller part of Vivian, a homeless woman addicted to crack cocaine (the cheaper version of cocaine that popularized drug use in the 1980s and 1990s). Vivian was also the girlfriend of Flipper's brother, Gator (who would be played by Samuel L. Jackson in the movie).

Halle was eager to stretch her acting chops in the dramatic role, but initially failed to convince Lee that she could play a crackhead. Lee, like most of the directors Halle had dealt with in the past, thought that Halle was too nice, too sweet, and too attractive to be believable in the part and refused to let her read for the role, even after she begged him for over an hour to give her a chance. Determined to prove she could be "real" enough to portray a foul-mouthed, combative drug addict, Halle famously scrubbed off all of her makeup, mussed up her hair, and went without bathing, brushing her teeth, and shaving her legs for days to prove that she could be grungy and unappealing enough to play the part convincingly. Impressed by Halle's dedication and tenacity, Lee gave her the part.

To prepare to play a desperate woman who is so strung out on drugs that she would do anything to pay for them (even, in one of the film's famous scenes, offer sexual favors in exchange for a few dollars to the main character as he walks his young daughter to her grade school), Halle took a job as a go-go dancer at a seedy strip club. However, she refused to go completely bare, so she had to pay the owner to let her dance while wearing a bikini and ended up handing over all of the tip money she had earned.[2] She also went on field trips with costar Samuel L. Jackson to Harlem neighborhoods that had been hit hard by the crack epidemic to add more realism to her portrayal. Jackson would later recall when he had met Halle for the first time. "Halle was this shy girl looking at the script saying, 'Can I say this? I can't talk like this?' I told her 'look, if you get through this, they will hire you to do whatever you want to do.' "[3]

When filming began, Halle immersed herself completely in the movie-making experience—continuing her stints of avoiding personal hygiene and studying everything that happened on the set, including shadowing Lee as he directed and turning up on days when she was not filming to watch the other actors work,[4] including legendary African-American actors Ossie Davis and Ruby Dee as they performed their heart-wrenching scenes playing Flipper's emotionally damaged parents. It was all a tremendous learning experience for the young actress, who was finally getting a taste of what it meant to work on a major motion picture and was looking forward to making even more.

It was not long before Halle got her wish. For years she had been struggling to find good roles in predominately White casts, but that all changed with the work of Spike Lee and the other African-American films that were released in 1991.

It was the year that African-American cinema experienced a renaissance of sorts, with several films written, directed by, and starring African-Americans on the screens. *Jungle Fever* was released in June, months after the debut of the critically acclaimed yet controversial movie *Boyz n the Hood* and weeks before *New Jack City*. Both movies were helmed by Black directors (John Singleton and Mario Van Peebles, respectively) and were widely seen by racially mixed audiences. While those films tackled the brutal effects of gang violence and organized drug dealing and were wildly popular with teenage moviegoers, *Jungle Fever* presented a nuanced portrayal of upper-middle-class Blacks in stark conflict with working-class Italian-Americans and was aimed at a decidedly adult audience. "With a potent mix of comedy and concern, 'Jungle Fever' scrambles toward a dissonant climax of hope and despair, carved out of anguish and an honest appraisal of the odds facing anyone who tries to bridge the chasm of race," wrote a critic in *Newsweek*.[5] The *New York Times* wrote,

> Make no mistake about it, "Jungle Fever" is a comedy, a big, visually splendid, serious social comedy that embraces the sorrowful as well as the hilarious. Mr. Lee was speaking from the heart in "Do the Right Thing," and made no attempt to hide it. "Jungle Fever" is no less deeply

felt, but the view is longer, the tone cooler, the command of technique so self-assured.[6]

While Halle's role was relatively small, her performance in *Jungle Fever* was very well received and gave her the chance to be taken seriously as a legitimate actress with a promising future. *Jungle Fever* went on to make over $32 million at the box office—an impressive haul for an independent film—and received plenty of buzz for its controversial subject matter and cinematic techniques.

But *Jungle Fever* was only one of three movies that put Halle Berry on the big screen in 1991: later that year, she had roles in two different movies that further showcased her range as an actress: *Strictly Business*, a romantic comedy that hit theaters in November, and *The Last Boy Scout*, a mainstream buddy movie teaming box-office superstar Bruce Willis (*Die Hard*, 1988) with comedian Damon Wayans (of the popular 1980s television sketch comedy show *In Living Color*, 1990–1994) that was released in December.

Strictly Business was a lighthearted comedic film with a predominately Black cast. The lead character, Waymon Tinsdale III (played by actor Joseph C. Phillips), is an uptight Buppie (Black urban professional) trying to climb to the top of the Manhattan real estate brokerage firm where he works. Waymon is all about keeping up appearances—as evidenced by his passionless relationship with Diedre, the uptight social climber that he had made his fiancée (played by Anne-Marie Johnson). Waymon's life is turned upside-down when he meets Natalie, the free-spirited hostess and nightclub promoter portrayed by Halle Berry. Natalie finds Waymon to be dull and uptight until their mutual friend Bobby (played by comedian Tommy David-son, another *In Living Color* alumni) gives him a hip makeover and teaches him how to unleash his cooler inner persona.

Even though it was a small-budget movie released to fewer theaters than most films, *Strictly Business* was considered a box-office disappointment, pulling in under $8 million in ticket sales. But Halle logged in more screen time in the film than in her other two roles that year combined, and the movie found a wider audience when it was released on video.

In *The Last Boy Scout*, her third movie of the year, Halle played Cory, a sexy nightclub dancer and sometime companion of Wayans's disgraced football player character. Bruce Willis played a former Secret Service agent that Cory hires to shadow her every move. After attempting to blackmail the football coach into resigning her boy-friend, Halle's character meets an untimely demise (courtesy of a mob hit squad) and the movie shifts into a buddy flick along the lines of *Lethal Weapon* (1987), the classic Mel Gibson/Danny Glover film released in 1987. Although Halle's scenes with Willis were minimal at best, it was her first shot at starring in a movie with an A-list actor. She would have a chance to play opposite Willis again later in her career.

Despite starring in more films in one year than most actors do in a lifetime, Halle expressed her frustration at what she called the "under-writing" of her characters in *Strictly Business* and *The Last Boy Scout*. Not one to merely play the cards she had been dealt, Halle tried to take matters into her own hands and write a script of her own:

> That's what inspired me to write my own things. That way, I'm in control, I'm holding the pen and paper. Black women need to put energy into their own projects—like Spike Lee, someone has got to be a pioneer and get it done, keep trying when doors are slammed in your face.[7]

Halle also expressed an interest at the time in becoming more like the strong, successful women she admired—women such as Oscar-winning actress/director Jodie Foster (*Taxi Driver*, 1976, and *The Silence of the Lambs*, 1991) and Angela Davis, an African-American social activist who was almost as famous for the resplendent oversized Afro hairstyle she proudly wore in the 1960s as she was for her radical politics. Halle told reporters on several occasions that she hoped to have the opportunity to play Davis in a movie one day.

Ambitious as ever, Halle tried to take matters into her own hands and create her own roles. She wrote a screenplay for a suspenseful thriller that she titled "Inside Out" and shopped it around to various studios with the same tenacity and persistence that she put into getting acting gigs. Unfortunately, no one was interested in her writing efforts, and Halle banished the script to the back of a drawer and rededicated herself to finding her next big part. This time, she would have better luck with a romantic comedy on the big screen and take a more serious turn in a high-profile return to the small screen.

BEAUTIFUL STAR RISING

Halle's star was definitely rising, and it was not just Hollywood insiders that were taking notice. The weekly national magazines *People* and *Us* both named Halle to their "Most Beautiful" lists in 1992, and she was the subject of several interviews and profiles.

That same year, she appeared in the Black romantic comedy *Boomerang*. The cast, led by comedian Eddie Murphy, was a who's who of Black Hollywood: Martin Lawrence, David Alan Grier, Robin Givens, Eartha Kitt, Grace Jones, Chris Rock, and Melvin Van Peebles were just some of the actors featured in the movie.

Murphy played Marcus Graham, a suave advertising executive and ladies' man who sets out to romance his attractive new boss, Jacqueline (played by Givens), and is surprised to find himself falling in love with her. He wants to settle down with her, but she is not interested in a commitment and scorns him for becoming emotionally attached. Rejected, Marcus finds solace with gal pal Angela Lewis, Halle's character. The two start out as platonic friends (Angela works in the art department of the firm where Marcus works and briefly dates one of Marcus's friends), but become romantically involved. Their relationship is in jeopardy when Jacqueline decides that she wants Marcus back.

The movie was an interesting choice for Murphy, who up until that point had starred in action films and star vehicles (*Beverly Hills Cop*, 1984, and *Coming to America*, 1988) that highlighted his often crass comedic prowess. The two movies he had been in prior to *Boomerang*— *Another 48 Hours* (1990) and *Harlem Nights* (1989)—were flops, so Murphy was in desperate need of a box-office hit.

In *Boomerang*, the jokes still came fast and furious, but Murphy revealed an ability to play a more sensitive character. For Halle, her role presented an opportunity to play a girlfriend role that had a little more depth and a lot more screen time than she had in *Strictly Business*, her previous attempt in the romantic comedy genre. Murphy's participation also gave the movie a high profile, and after it was released in theaters in July 1992, *Boomerang* went on to earn over $131 million worldwide.

While most of the attention on the film was lavished on Murphy's and Givens's performances, Halle did not go unnoticed. "Berry is so warm and charming you want to cuddle her," wrote famous film critic Roger Ebert in his review of the film.[8] "Berry is alluring throughout," said *Variety* movie critic Lawrence Cohn.[9]

QUEEN ON THE SMALL SCREEN

A six-hour miniseries, *Queen*, was based on the unfinished novel of the same name by Pulitzer Prize–winning author Alex Haley. Haley was still working on the book when he died in February 1992. His previous book, *Roots*, told the complicated tale of Kunta Kinte, an African brought to America from Africa and was based on Haley's own research into his family's history. When *Roots* aired in 1977 on CBS, it was a history-making television event, pulling in millions of riveted viewers and earning a Golden Globe for Best Television Drama.

Halle was cast in the title role of Queen, but it was another part that she had to fight for. The producers thought that, at age 23, the actress was too young to play a character that goes from age 15 to 50 throughout the course of the miniseries. Halle, who strongly identified with the half-Black, half-White character of Queen, was not about to take no for an answer. To convince producer Mark Wolper that she was willing to work hard to play the role, she bought her own plane ticket from New York to Los Angeles and picked up the tab for her cabs and hotels in order to take a screen test. Her performance won the makers of the miniseries over, and Halle was offered the role.

The story of *Queen* begins with Easter (played by Jasmine Guy), a character based on Haley's great-grandmother on his father's side. A slave on a big plantation in Alabama, the beautiful, light-skinned Easter falls in love with her master, James (Tim Daly), a White man of Irish descent. However, the times did not allow for an interracial love affair to blossom, and her master ends up in an arranged marriage with a wealthy White woman. However, his love affair with Easter continues in secret, and the two have a daughter, Queen. When Easter dies, Queen becomes the maid of her half-sister.

After her father goes off to fight in the Civil War, Queen fights to be accepted by her White relatives, who want nothing to do with her. Now orphaned by the Black side of her family, Queen is forced to fend for herself. She endures hardship and sorrow before finding love, getting married, and having children. The sweeping saga follows Queen

from the antebellum South to the twentieth century and provides a
fresh look at the complicated dynamics that have existed between
Blacks and Whites in America for centuries.

The challenging role was a difficult one for Halle to play. It was
physically demanding, and the actress at one point fell off a horse and
injured her back, shutting down production for 10 days and requiring
that the actress get shots of cortisone and take prescription pain pills
to get through the rest of the filming. Actor Danny Glover, who played
Halle's husband in the project, famously came close to walking off the
set rather than wait for filming to resume.[10]

Halle also had to draw upon all of her previous experience and
acting lessons to play a woman from young adulthood to old age.
The lessons her mother taught her early on about what it meant to
be a woman of mixed race living in America and how to deal with
not being accepted by either race also factored into Halle's prepara-
tions for the role. The experience of playing a woman who is
emotionally tormented, physically abused, and called repeated racial
epithets to her face was almost too much for Halle to bear. By the
time that filming on the series had reached its completion, Halle
was emotionally spent and referred to herself as a wreck that no one
wanted to be around:

> I really felt the injustice and I was called nigger just one time too many
> on screen. It was all too much and after three-and-a-half months on the
> shoot I began to take it too personally, which you don't want to do, but
> if you're a sensitive human being who has emotions and feelings then
> it's difficult not to let some of those tears be real.[11]

Her emotional ordeal on-screen was matched by an equally trauma-
tizing episode in her personal life: a relationship she had with a man
she had been dating turned sour, and allegedly took a violent turn.
Having recalled what it was like to watch her mother be abused,
and remembering her mother's advice that she should never stay with
a man who hit her, Halle left her boyfriend for good after that one
incident. Unfortunately, the physical damage was permanent:
Halle lost 80 percent of the hearing in her left ear.[12] She reportedly
sought the help of a therapist, who helped her move past the incident
and come back to reality after becoming so wrapped up in playing
Queen.

When the miniseries (which cost $15 million to make) finally aired in February 1993, 30 million viewers tuned in. The reviews were mixed, but most critics recognized Halle's efforts. "Halle Berry's Queen sometimes falters," wrote a critic for the *Christian Science Monitor*. "It is a very large and very difficult role for so young an actress. Yet she has her moments—moments that are profoundly moving and richly revealing."[13] Halle would win an NAACP Image Award for Outstanding Lead Actress in a Television Movie, Mini-Series, or Dramatic Special for her role in *Queen*.

MORE ROLES, MORE CHALLENGES

The buzz created by *Queen* increased Halle's star power, and she was offered more roles starring opposite popular A-list actors. The summer of 1993 would see Halle back on the big screen—in the Patrick Swayze–vehicle *Father Hood* and the teenage football drama *The Program*, which starred James Caan (*The Godfather*, 1972).

In *Father Hood*, Swayze played Jack Charles, an escaped con and small-time criminal who takes his kids on the run as he tries to evade the FBI and the local police in four different states. Halle costarred as Kathleen Mercer, an investigative reporter trying to hunt him down. It fizzled in the theaters, earning a lukewarm $3.4 million at the box office.

The Program, a football drama starring Caan as the coach of a diverse group of college football players at a top-ranked university, fared slightly better. Most of the players have issues—the quarterback is an alcoholic, another player is using steroids, and yet another is caught cheating. Halle played Autumn Winters, a pretty coed who tutors one of the freshmen players (Omar Epps) and ends up being caught in the middle of a love triangle. "Halle Berry is perhaps 'The Program's' most underutilized strength," wrote one critic. "She's the best thing in the picture, but has little to do, and certainly nothing that stretches her abilities."[14]

The movie got more attention for a scene depicting the players lying in traffic while cars roar past them (the scene was later cut after real-life imitators were killed reenacting the stunt) than it did for its story line or performances. It went on to make $23 million, making a respectable but less than anticipated amount of money at the box office.

SOME THINGS CHANGE, WHILE OTHERS STAY THE SAME

For Halle, it was a time filled with parties, premieres, and press for her numerous films. It was a whirlwind of professional opportunities; even though all of her movies were not box office gold, she was being seen and taken seriously by some of Hollywood's heavy hitters. She was starting to have more choices and being placed in an enviable position to not have to leap at everything she was offered. She passed on a role in *Waiting to Exhale* (1995—singer Whitney Houston and actress Angela Bassett were among those who said yes to the film) because she did not agree with the director's vision of the character. But that choosiness may have also cost her the role of a lifetime: Halle made a famous misstep when she turned down the role of Annie Porter, the female lead in the summer blockbuster action film *Speed* (1994). Sandra Bullock, then a virtually unknown actress, would take the role instead (starring opposite Keanu Reeves and Dennis Hopper). That film made Bullock an A-list star and made over $250 million. Halle would later admit that passing up the role was a dumb move.[15]

But still, after all of the progress she had made, there were some doors that were still closed: Halle desperately wanted to read for the lead role in *Indecent Proposal* (1993), but was not even allowed to audition (the part went to Demi Moore). At the time, Halle complained that the producers would not even consider her because she was Black and the role was written for a White woman married to a White man and desired by another White man.[16]

DATING IN THE PUBLIC EYE

Becoming a famous celebrity made it hard—if not impossible—for Halle to meet and date a "regular" guy, and she began dating men that her fame allowed her to meet. While Halle herself has not confirmed many of these relationships, the Hollywood rumor mill linked Halle to her *Jungle Fever* costar, Wesley Snipes, actor and comedian Eddie Murphy, rhythm-and-blues singer Christopher Williams, and Danny Wood, a member of the 1990s pop supergroup New Kids on the Block.

Halle would quickly learn what other celebrities already knew: that success can make it hard to meet the right person, that the tabloids would write lies and innuendos, and that even the most casual of photos taken with a member of the opposite sex could quickly be misconstrued as an illicit affair. Halle did her best to keep her private life private, despite the paparazzi's cravings for juicy gossip, and tried not to take the rumors personally.

As Halle's fame intensified, so would the public's interest in her. It was a heady time: she was starting to make more money, and it was increasingly more difficult for her to venture out in public without being recognized, even followed on occasion.

But it was also a time in which she would meet the man that she would call her husband, a handsome outfielder for the Atlanta Braves who would change the course of her life.

NOTES

1. "Playing the Part," *Montreal Gazette*, April 10, 2007.

2. Barbara Davies, "A Star against All Odds," *Daily Mail* (London), May 19, 2007.

3. Hollywood Walk of Fame ceremony.

4. "Berry Almost Chooses Bylines over Marquees," *Toronto Star*, April 13, 2007.

5. "Spiking a Fever," *Newsweek*, June 10, 1991.

6. "Spike Lee's Comedy of Sorrow," *New York Times*, June 7, 1991.

7. "Halle Berry Shifts into Hollywood's Fast Lane," *USA Today*, November 20, 1991.

8. Roger Ebert, *Boomerang* review, *Chicago Sun-Times*, July 1, 1992.

9. Lawrence Cohn, "Boomerang," *Variety*, June 29, 1992.

10. "Halle Berry's Reign," *USA Today*, July 10, 1992.

11. "Halle Berry, Star of the New 'Roots' Saga, Talks about the Personal Agony of her Role," *Daily Mail* (London), October 3, 1993.

12. Ibid.

13. M. S. Masom, "Complex World of 'Queen,'" *Christian Science Monitor*, February 9, 1993.

14. James Berardinelli, ReelViews Web site, http://www.reelviews.net/movies.php.

15. "For Halle Berry, Hollywood Still Hasn't Overcome," *USA Today*, March 14, 1996.

16. Ibid.

Halle Berry, Miss USA, is shown in costume at a Variety Club of Great Britain luncheon at the Hilton Hotel in London, England, Friday, November 7, 1986. The 20-year old student from Cleveland, Ohio, said her national costume, by American designer Dick Frank, reflects "America's advancement in space." AP Photo/Dave Caulkin

Halle Berry shows off her Oscar backstage after winning for best actress for her role in Monster's Ball during the 74th annual Academy Awards on Sunday, March 24, 2002, in Los Angeles. AP Photo/Doug Mills

Actress Halle Berry accepts the award for Outstanding Supporting Actress in a Motion Picture for her role in Die Another Day at the NAACP Image Awards, in Los Angeles, Saturday, March 8, 2003. AP Photo/Lucy Nicholson

Halle Berry arrives at the 16th annual "Carousel of Hope" Benefit for Childhood Diabetes at the Beverly Hilton Hotel in Beverly Hills, California, Saturday, October, 23, 2004. The event is a fund-raiser founded by Barbara and Marvin Davis to benefit the Barbara Davis Center for Childhood Diabetes in Denver. AP Photo/Jason Merritt

Actress Halle Berry stands on top of her star on the Hollywood Walk of Fame in Los Angeles, Tuesday, April 3, 2007, after the induction ceremony. AP Photo/Kevork Djansezian

Halle Berry arrives at the 19th annual Palm Springs International Film Festival Awards Gala in Palm Springs, California, on Saturday, January 5, 2008. AP Photo/Matt Sayles

Actress Halle Berry poses on the press line at the Silver Rose Gala held at the Beverly Hills Hotel in Beverly Hills, California, on Sunday, April 27, 2008. AP Photo/Dan Steinberg

Actress Halle Berry at the 15th Annual Entertainment Industry Foundation Revlon Run/Walk For Women in Los Angeles on Saturday, May 10, 2008. AP Photo/Dan Steinberg

Halle Berry arrives at Elle's 15th annual Women in Hollywood event in Los Angeles on Monday, October 6, 2008. AP Photo/Matt Sayles

Actress Halle Berry arrives at the premiere of the feature film The
Soloist *in Los Angeles on Monday, April 20, 2009.* AP Photo/Dan
Steinberg

Chapter 4

TOUGH BREAKS

A SUCCESSFUL BLIND DATE

David Justice was a handsome home-run hitter with three Major League Baseball seasons under his belt when he was being interviewed by Conrad Clowers, a freelance newspaper journalist, in 1992. The two developed an easy rapport, and Justice, 1990 National League Rookie of the Year who was playing for the Atlanta Braves, casually mentioned to Clowers that if he ever met Halle Berry, he would marry her in a second. At the time, the single Justice was considered to be one of Atlanta's most eligible bachelors, so talk of marriage peaked the writer's interest. As circumstances would have it, Clowers told Justice that he had been trying to get an interview with Halle for months—and that if he ever scored a sit-down with the actress, he promised to put in a good word for Justice. Justice laughed him off, dismissing both the interview and a date as long-shot propositions for both men.

Clowers got his wish when Halle was filming the movie *Boomerang* (1992). Toward the end of his one-on-one interview, he asked Halle if she was interested in baseball and whether she had heard of Justice. Berry's interest peaked—not only did she know Justice's name, but she had seen him on television and recalled that she thought he was cute. Halle obliged Clowers's request to autograph a photo of herself to give to Justice—and penned her phone number onto the glossy portrait below her signature.

Justice called Halle, and several more phone conversations followed. They discovered they had a lot in common: they both were born and raised in Ohio (Halle in Cleveland, Justice in Cincinnati) and had been abandoned by their fathers at an early age. When the two finally met in person after a Braves game, it was love at first sight. It was not long before they were spotted together out on dates and at public events, looking very much enamored with one another.

Eight short months after they first met, it was Halle who asked Justice to marry her. The two tied the knot in Atlanta in a private ceremony on New Year's Day in 1993.[1] It is not known if any of their friends or family members attended the wedding, and no photos were ever released.

In a decidedly modern twist, they decided to declare their love with his-and-hers tattoos: Justice had Halle's name tattooed on his arm, and Halle had his name inked into her rear end.[2] Halle famously appeared as a guest on the *Late Show with David Letterman* and showed her tattoo to Letterman (but not to the audience). Against the conventional advice of the time, they decided to get married without a prenuptial agreement.

David Justice and Halle Berry made a glamorous pair, the beautiful Hollywood starlet and the handsome professional baseball player, and comparisons were often made to another high-profile actress/athlete couple from another era: Marilyn Monroe and Joe DiMaggio. In a parallel situation with their famous predecessors, Halle and Justice were hounded by the paparazzi and became the subject of hundreds of magazine articles and television news segments.

The twosome was very supportive of each other's careers, and Justice credited their marriage with keeping him grounded and focused on playing baseball. "We're on the same level," Justice said of his wife. "There are so many correlations in our lives. Recognition everywhere. Being in the spotlight. The same pressures it carries. We can relate."[3] But he was not too busy to look after his wife: on Wednesday, June 23, 1993, Halle fell ill and was admitted to the hospital to undergo a procedure. Justice left his team behind in Philadelphia to be by her side.[4] His team granted him permission to leave for "personal reasons," and he returned in time to make the game the following Tuesday.

Halle made every effort to step into her new role as a ballplayer's wife: she traveled with her husband to his games and was seen sitting with the other wives at the playoffs. She made every effort to turn their Atlanta house into a comfortable, luxurious home (they also maintained a home in the Hollywood Hills area of Los Angeles). However, her career beckoned, and she left to film another pivotal role.

FIGHTING HARD FOR A "LOSING" ROLE

Director Stephen Gyllenhaal (father of actors Jake and Maggie, and director of *A Dangerous Woman*, 1993), like many Hollywood veterans, was having a hard time imagining that Halle Berry was capable of deepening her range as an actress. So when he received word that Halle wanted to audition for a leading role in his latest movie, he agreed to see her, but only as a courtesy. "I saw nothing in her work that suggested she could do this . . . I assumed she couldn't handle it."[5]

Losing Isaiah (1995), which was based on a novel of the same name that was published in 1993 by author Seth J. Margolis, was inspired by true events. The role of Khalia Richards was a hotly contested one—every Black actress in Hollywood wanted the role. Gyllenhaal had already auditioned several contenders when Halle expressed an interest.

Perhaps the fact that Halle and the director both hailed from Cleveland opened the door a little wider. Halle would audition several times for the part of Khalia, a crack addict who abandons her baby son, Isaiah, in a cardboard box with the trash and thinks he had died. It turns out that the child entered the foster system and was eventually adopted by a passionate social worker (played by Jessica Lange, herself a former model turned actress). Three years later, Khalia turns her life around, gets clean, finds out that her son is alive, and fights to regain custody of her son.

Losing Isaiah explores the delicate issues of race, family, and parenthood. Samuel L. Jackson would appear with his *Jungle Fever* (1991) costar once again, this time playing Khalia's lawyer, a public-interest attorney. Actors David Strathairn (*Good Night and Good Luck*, 2005) and Cuba Gooding, Jr. (Academy Award Winner for *Jerry Maguire*, 1996) also played supporting roles.

To delve into the character's psyche and prove that she had the acting chops to handle the role, Halle tapped deep into her reservoir of experiences and emotions, a technique that is commonly known as method acting. Her resolve eventually won Gyllenhaal over, so while Halle's husband was traveling the country trying to help his team get to the World Series, she made a solo trip to Chicago and spent four long months on the movie shoot.

Her hard work paid off when the movie was released a year later and reviews were decidedly mixed; some thought the film was too weepy and overwrought: "Berry, whose talents are competent, makes the transition from ghetto citizen to reformed citizen a bit too neatly," wrote a critic in the *San Francisco Chronicle*.[6] Other reviewers who saw the film praised it as a brave portrayal of a complicated and emotional social issue. Another critic railed about the storyline. "The narrative is too fragmented and the film's point of view shifts for stretches that are too lengthy—initially it feels like Berry's story, then for a long period it's Lange's, then it's Berry's again," he wrote.[7]

Positive reviews praised Halle's performance. "As Khalia reads from an adult primer about the effects of drugs on the fetuses of pregnant women, Berry registers her character's belated metamorphosis from crack head to responsible mother. She is shattering," wrote one critic.[8] "It's a heart-wrenching portrayal, with an underpinning of willfulness that radiates in every close-up," wrote another.[9] The movie may have been too serious for most moviegoers's tastes: the worldwide gross was less than $9 million, far below the estimated $17 million it cost to make the film.

YABBA-DABBA GIRL

Halle's next film project would see her take a decidedly comedic and lighthearted turn. *The Flintstones* was a beloved Hanna-Barbera kid's cartoon that aired original episodes on television on the ABC network from 1960 to 1966. It depicted the lives of Fred Flintstone, a hard-working family man, his wife, Wilma, and their friends, Barney and Betty, as they lived in the Stone Age, worked in a rock quarry, and rode to work in cars powered by their feet. A live-action version of the series had been batted around Hollywood for decades; the project finally got the green light in the early 1990s. More than 30 writers famously labored on *The Flintstones'* screenplay, and director Steven Spielberg served as one of the movie's producers. In keeping with the cartoon's spirit, Spielberg's name was listed in the credits as Steven Spielrock.

John Goodman was cast as Fred, Elizabeth Perkins as Wilma, Rick Moranis as Barney, and Rosie O'Donnell played Betty. Halle was cast in the role of Rosetta Stone, a tantalizing vixen who works for Fred's boss, Cliff Vandercave (Kyle MacLachlan), and conspires to use Fred's lack of smarts to help them steal money from their company ("Berry is slinky as his seductive aide-de-camp," wrote *Variety*.[10] Halle's role was small but memorable as she sashays across the screen in a fur bikini and makes Fred Flintstone weak in the knees.

The movie was visually dazzling—no expense was spared to recreate the prehistoric cartoon world in three stunning dimensions—and appealed to a new generation of children and also adults who were nostalgic for their favorite childhood cartoon (Halle was a fan of the series herself when she was growing up).

A marketing blitz preceded the film's release: The studio, Universal Pictures, spent more money promoting *The Flintstones* (1994) than it did on *Jurassic Park* (1993). The fast-food restaurant chain McDonald's did a promotional tie-in (and was depicted in the film as "RocDonald's"), and socks, jackets, and ties bearing the film's characters and logos were sold in department stores.[11] The film company also signed a deal with toy company Mattel Inc. to create toys based on the characters, but a Rosetta Stone doll was not created. "As I understand it, you usually have the bad guys and the good guys, so the kids can hold them in each hand and fight," said the film's director, Brian Levant. "What would you do with a Halle Berry doll?"[12] Halle, for her part, said that she did not feel slighted that her character did not have a doll.

Hopes were indeed high when *The Flintstones* opened in theaters nationwide in February 1994. It was met with equal amounts of anticipation and hype, and while it made a good showing, it was not the blockbuster that Universal Studios was hoping it would be. The film was produced for $45 million and made $131 million at the U.S. box office.

A MARRIAGE FALLS APART

Justice was at his wife's side at the red-carpet premiere of *The Flintstones*, but three weeks later, Halle would be gone again. This time, she was off to Africa to film her role in the television movie *Solomon and Sheba* (1995) in Morocco. Based on the story in the Old Testament of the Bible, Halle played Nikhaule, the Queen of Sheba, in the tale opposite Jimmy Smits in the role of King Solomon. The movie, which aired on the cable network Showtime, depicted their romance and the queen's sudden rise to power. ("Enchanting," said the *New York Amsterdam News* of her performance.)[13]

Halle's career was moving full speed ahead, and Justice had great seasons playing for the Braves, placing third in the Most Valuable Player votes in 1993 and leading his team to a World Series championship in 1995. But somewhere along the line, their relationship soured. They were spending an increasing amount of time away from one another and had begun to drift apart. A spark of hope was lit when they went to Bermuda to celebrate their third anniversary and attempt to repair their relationship. Halle thought they could work out their issues and emerge as a stronger couple, but Justice, apparently, did not see things the same way:

> We were going to go home and really give it a try . . . the marriage could work if we both wanted it to. I believed that. I passed up a movie so I could go to spring training with David and try to invest the time in us. And then one day he came home and said, 'I don't want to be married.' When I realized he was really serious and there was nothing I could do, the next day I packed my things, and I went back to my home in L.A.[14]

They had been living apart for months before they decided to make their split official. After 38 months of marriage, on February 24, 1996, David Justice and Halle Berry announced their plans to divorce. Their split seemed amicable at first, with David announcing graciously during an interview at training camp that he still loved Halle and wished her all the best.[15] Halle, for her part, released a statement that she was not prepared to discuss the painful and private situation[16] and refused to comment on an incident the week before in which Justice was pulled over by cops in an area in Riviera Beach, Florida, that was known for drug trafficking and prostitutes (Justice later defended himself by saying that he had stopped in the area only because he was lost, and no charges were filed).[17]

However, the niceties quickly evaporated when Halle filed for divorce in 1996 in California, a community property state that splits the assets of separating couples equally. Justice was incensed by Halle's decision and felt that it was an attempt by his estranged wife to take all of his money. Justice filed a countersuit in Georgia, a state with laws that support a more equitable division of property based on salaries and assets before the marriage began, among other considerations.[18] He also told a reporter that Halle "wasn't the same person I was with before we got married" and that she carried a lot of baggage from her previous relationships.[19] Halle, meanwhile, accused Justice of cheating on her and being abusive.[20] Justice denied her allegations. Things came to a boiling point when Halle asked a Los Angeles judge for a restraining order, alleging that Justice came to her home one morning and threatened to break all of the windows in her home. The incident occurred after Justice showed up unannounced to pick up some of his belongings and Halle refused to let him in.[21]

FOCUSING ON HER CAREER

Despite all of the personal turmoil that she had to deal with, Halle had films to promote. She was in three movies in 1996—smaller roles in *Executive Decision* and *Race the Sun* and a starring role in *The Rich Man's Wife*. *Executive Decision* was a big-budget action flick starring Kurt Russell and Steven Seagal in which Halle played Jean, a flight attendant on an airplane taken over by Islamic terrorists and filled with nerve gas. The terrorists plan to blow the plane up over Washington, D.C., to disperse the gas, and kill millions of people. A military team is sent in to board the plane in midair and rescue the civilians, and Halle helps the rescuers in their fight against the terrorists.

At that time, Halle's star power was enough to get her second billing in the movie's trailer, but she did not appear on posters for the film—a move that was seen as a snub given the size of her role. But *Executive Decision* did perform fairly well, earning $134 million at the box office.

Race the Sun was an altogether different kind of movie. Based on a true story, the PG-rated, family-friendly film told the story of a group of high school misfits in Hawaii who develop an interest in science. The students learn to work as a team as they build a solar-powered car. Halle played the leading role of Miss Sandra Beecher, the new teacher who inspires the students and takes them and their car to compete in a prestigious race in Australia.

Race the Sun was a small film that did not find a large audience, but it was compared to a couple of classic school-based dramas: *To Sir, With Love* (1967, with actor Sidney Poitier in the title role) and *Dangerous Minds* (1995, starring Michelle Pfeiffer).

Halle's next role would be a dramatic one that allowed her to show off her dramatic acting skills. In *The Rich Man's Wife*, she was cast in the starring role of Josie Potenza, a woman trapped in a bad marriage to a wealthy man. Josie discovers that their prenuptial agreement would leave her penniless if she divorced her cheating, alcoholic husband, so one night she conspires with a stranger to have him killed. The taunting thriller, which also starred actors Clive Owen (*Duplicity*, 2009) and Peter Greene (*Pulp Fiction*, 1994), was a star vehicle for Halle, but it made only a disappointing $8.5 million in ticket sales.

HITTING BOTTOM

Halle put on a brave face while promoting her work and reading for her next projects, but privately, she was distraught over the breakup of her marriage and the nastiness of the divorce proceedings. Halle's mother, Judith, flew out to support her daughter during the difficult time, and the actress's close friends rallied around her. Still, Halle recalls that it was one of the lowest periods of her life. She put on a brave face to convince her loved ones that she was all right, but her self-esteem was shattered. Halle hit bottom one day when she walked out to her garage with her dogs and got in her car. She had every intention of turning the key in the ignition and remaining in that car until it filled with carbon monoxide from the exhaust fumes, which would cause her to pass out and eventually die. She thought it would be painless, a mess-free way to end it all.[22]

She could not do it. No matter how much Halle was hurting, she did not really want to end her life. Halle turned off the ignition, got out of the car, got into therapy, and, slowly but surely, learned to move past her failed marriage.[23]

COMING OUT OF THE DARK

Halle's divorce from David Justice was finalized in 1997, and the terms were kept confidential. It was time for Halle to put her focus back on her career, and she started off the year promoting *B.A.P.S.*, a comedy directed by Robert Townsend (*Hollywood Shuffle*, 1987) that was different from anything else she had ever done.

The term "B.A.P.S." is short for Black American Princesses—it is a play on "J.A.P.S.," a term used to refer to materialistic Jewish-American women who are raised in privilege and adopt a flashy, pampered lifestyle. Halle played Nisi, a ghetto-fabulous, trash-talking, gold tooth–wearing homegirl living in Decatur, Georgia, who travels to Los Angeles with her friend, Mickey (Natalie Desselle), to compete in the Video Dance Girl of the World contest. While waiting in line to audition (a scene in which Halle famously wore a shiny, skintight orange jumpsuit and a blonde weave that looked like a gigantic pineapple), the girls are approached by the director's nephew, who says he is casting for a music video and offers to pay them $10,000. When they arrive at a fancy mansion, they are told that they have really been hired to look after the nephew's elderly uncle, Mr. Blakemore (Martin Landeau). The girls are like fish out of water, but they discover their true selves in their new, fancy surroundings and teach Mr. Blakemore to enjoy life again and help him avoid the schemes of his nephew, who is trying to steal his fortune.

While some critics defended Halle's performance ("The movie is good-spirited and Berry throws herself into the slapstick with ease and enthusiasm," wrote a critic for the *New York Daily News*),[24] most of them professed a strong dislike of *B.A.P.S.* and many said the movie perpetuated ugly stereotypes about African-American women. "Jaw-droppingly bad, a movie so misconceived I wonder why anyone involved wanted to make it," wrote critic Roger Ebert in his assessment of the film, going on to say, "The actresses don't inhabit the caricatures with conviction. The result is a hurtful stereotype, because the comedy doesn't work to redeem it." Speaking in her own defense, Halle said that she did not want to look stupid; rather, she was trying to be funny.[25]

After a less-than-stellar opening weekend (under $3 million in ticket sales, far below what is considered to be a good sign), the movie languished in the theaters for a few months before it was pulled. The infamous orange jumpsuit that Halle wore in the film was donated to Planet Hollywood, a chain of restaurants with a movie-memorabilia theme and celebrity investors (including Arnold Schwarzenegger and Sylvester Stallone) that were popular tourist destinations in the 1990s.

A DATE WITH OPRAH

When Halle had lived in Chicago in the late 1980s, she had no doubt heard of Oprah Winfrey, the enigmatic local talk-show host who would rise to international prominence when her show went into national syndication in 1986. Oprah was a local legend long before the rest of the world had heard of her, and as a powerful, successful African-American woman, she was undoubtedly a role model for Halle.

In 1989, Halle would have her first opportunity to work with Oprah when she was cast in *Oprah Winfrey Presents: The Wedding*, a two-part television miniseries based on the novel by Dorothy West, who was the last surviving member of the Harlem Renaissance, a group of writers, poets, and artists who rose to prominence in the 1930s. Richard Wright and Langston Hughes were some of her more famous contemporaries.

Oprah produced the movie through her production company, Harpo Films. Halle played Shelby Coles, a privileged young woman born into a wealthy, bourgeoisie family during the 1950s. Shelby and her mother (Lynn Whitfield) are in the middle of planning Shelby's elaborate wedding in Martha's Vineyard to Meade Howell (Eric Thal), a White musician who is struggling to make ends meet. While his financial status is socially undesirable, the match is approved by Shelby's White grandmother, who wants to keep the family bloodline as Caucasian as possible. Her plans are threatened when Lute, a dark-skinned African-American widower with three kids, rolls into town and attempts to seduce Shelby. "Two men. Two different worlds. One final decision," read the subtitle for the movie, which shone a light on the rarely seen world of the Black upper-class in the United States.

"It's about family," Halle said of the plot.

> It's about people accepting one another for who they are, not for the color of their skin, or how much money they have, or how educated they are. It's really about dealing from the heart. Expressing love no matter what color you are, or what "class" of people you belong to.[26]

The Wedding aired on ABC on February 22 and 23, 1998, and made a respectable showing in the Nielsen ratings.

ANOTHER SHOT AT SATIRE

A year after Halle endured the hard knocks from critics and the movie-going public for her role in *B.A.P.S.*, she appeared in *Bulworth* (1998), a dark comedy about an incumbent California senator (played by Warren Beatty) who has become dissatisfied with American politics and decides he does not want to live anymore—so he puts a "hit" out on himself. He also seizes the opportunity in the time before he is supposed to be assassinated to tell people exactly what he thinks by rapping his speeches—a move that should have destroyed his career, but instead makes him more popular than ever. During the three days he has left to live, he meets Nina (Halle Berry), a young woman from the inner city who shows him the harsh realities of her existence and with whom the senator becomes romantically involved. Actors Don Cheadle, Oliver Platt, Christine Baranski, and Isaiah Washington also had roles in the film.

Bulworth was a risky choice for Halle, but Beatty, who had chosen her for the role, convinced her to do it. Her gamble paid off with mixed results. "Despite Berry's personal allure, [her] character's inscrutability often serves as a drain on the action," wrote a critic for *Variety*.[27] "This political satire that's as fresh and exhilarating as anything we've seen come out of Hollywood in quite some time," opined another newspaper critic.[28]

While the film was widely praised for its unflinching look at the American political process, it was not exactly a hit with moviegoers. Made for $30 million, it grossed less than $27 million at the box office.

A "FOOL" IN LOVE ON-SCREEN

Halle would have better luck with a biopic based on the life of a legendary doo-wop singer. In *Why Do Fools Fall in Love*, Halle played Zola Taylor, a member of the 1950s rhythm-and-blues group The Platters. She falls in love with Frankie Lymon, a charismatic young singer whose biggest chart-topper was the song of the movie's title and who later died of a heroin overdose.

The movie is told in flashbacks from the 1980s, when Zola and Frankie's other two wives (played by Vivica A. Fox and Lela Rochon) sued their ex-husband's estate for the right to his money and fought with each other over who should get the lion's share and which one was more beloved by Frankie. Halle played the elegant singer with class and grace, giving a hint of what was to come when she would play another, more iconic performer nearly a decade later.

A TRIUMPHANT RETURN TO MODELING

Halle was sure she had left her modeling days behind her for good when Revlon came calling in 1997. The cosmetics company, founded in 1932, was looking to hire actresses, not models, to promote its affordable yet high-quality line of drugstore makeup and approached Halle to become one of its new "faces" to help reflect the diversity of the brand. Halle accepted Revlon's offer and signed a multimillion dollar deal to appear in commercials and print advertisements alongside fellow actresses Salma Hayek, Julianne Moore, Daisy Fuentes, Kim Delaney, and Melanie Griffith.

A curly-haired Halle was featured in ads by herself for Revlon's MoistureStay Lipcolor, Super Lustrous Lipstick, and other makeup products. In one memorable ad, Halle is featured in her signature short, spiky haircut and a black knit top that accentuated her upper back. No products are shown, but on the bottom of the ad are the words "Revlon. Be Unforgettable." The campaign further cemented Halle's status as a mainstream beauty icon who needed no introduction: her famous face was immediately recognizable to millions of people worldwide.

DOROTHY DANDRIDGE'S INFLUENCE ON HALLE'S LIFE

Halle has often mentioned that the actress who had the most influence on her career was an African-American woman who also hailed from Cleveland. Dorothy Jean Dandridge was born on November 9, 1922, the second daughter (Vivian was born in 1921) of aspiring singer and actress Ruby Dandridge and Cyril Dandridge, a minister and cabinetmaker from whom Ruby separated shortly before Dorothy's birth. Ruby channeled her ambitions into her daughters, creating an act for them that she dubbed "The Wonder Children" that toured throughout the southern United States (appearing on what was famously referred to as the "Chitlin' Circuit") for five years. The girls went out on the road while their mother stayed behind in Cleveland to work as a performer.

When the Great Depression hit and gigs in Cleveland and on the Chitlin' Circuit became scarce, Ruby packed up the girls and relocated to Los Angeles, where she was able to find steady work in Hollywood playing mostly small parts as maids and cooks in films. She continued to push the stage careers of Vivian and Dorothy, who had renamed their act "The Dandridge Sisters" and performed at such notable venues as the Apollo Theater in Harlem, New York.

Dorothy's career would soon eclipse that of her sister. Dorothy's first on-screen appearance was in a short *Our Gang* film at the tender age of 13. Two years later, in 1935, Dorothy had a small role in the Marx Brothers film *A Day at the Races*. Larger roles as a murderer in *Four Shall Die* (1940) and *Drums of the Congo* (1942) followed, but it was her skills as a nightclub performer that won her acclaim. On the personal front, Dorothy married legendary tap dancer Harold Nicholas (who performed as half of the Nicholas Brothers with his sibling Fayard) in 1942.

During the six years that she was married to Nicholas, Dorothy practically retired from the entertainment business to become a full-time wife. In 1943, she gave birth to a daughter, Harolyn Suzanne, who was severely brain damaged and required constant care. Dorothy reluctantly placed her in full-time foster care.

After her divorce from Harold, Dorothy returned to work, landing a coveted role as the title character in the musical *Carmen Jones* (1954). Written and directed by Otto Preminger (with whom it is widely rumored that Dorothy had a turbulent affair), the movie featured an all-Black cast, including Harry Belafonte, Pearl Bailey, Diahann Carroll, and Joe Adams. While Dandridge originally sang her own songs, her voice was considered to be not good enough and was dubbed over by opera singer Marilyn Horne.

However, Dandridge's electrifying performance shone through, and the film was a critical and box-office success. The role made her the first African-American actress to be nominated for an Academy Award in the Best Actress category and only the third African-American actress to be nominated for an Academy Award in any category (Hattie McDaniel won for her supporting role as Mammy in 1939's *Gone With the Wind*, and Ethel Waters was nominated for her role in the 1949 film *Pinky*).

Dandridge did not win the Academy Award (actress Grace Kelly took home the statue for her role in *Country Girl*, 1954), but she continued to act in films (most notably in the film adaptation of the 1959 musical *Porgy & Bess*) and perform in nightclubs. She married one more time, in 1959, to restauranteur Jack Denison and divorced him in 1962.

After she discovered that her financial handlers had stolen a significant amount of her money and left her in debt to the government for unpaid back taxes, Dandridge was forced to sell her house and had a nervous breakdown. Just as she was on the verge of making a comeback, Dandridge would tragically die in 1965 at the young age of 42 after accidentally overdosing on antidepressants.

Despite Dandridge's tragic and early death, her legacy as a groundbreaking and courageous entertainer endures. Dandridge bravely stood up to racial prejudice and opened the doors of opportunity to the generations of African-American actresses that would follow in her footsteps—including Halle Berry. Dandridge's life story would continue to fascinate people as several books were authored in the years following her death.

THE BATTLE TO PLAY DOROTHY DANDRIDGE

In the 1990s, one of the hottest projects in town looked as if it was finally going to be a reality: a biopic depicting the life of Dorothy Dandridge, the legendary African-American singer and actress. A Dandridge film had come close to being made several times before, with pop singer and sometime actress Janet Jackson under serious consideration to play the role of Dandridge. Jackson even went as far as portraying a Dandridge-like heroine in one of her music videos, for the song "Twenty Foreplay," in 1995. Jackson's Dandridge film project eventually ran out of steam, and dozens of African-American actresses once again lined up to compete with one another. Halle was among them; she auditioned several times, only to be turned down over and over again.

One version of the Dandridge script was eventually purchased by Whitney Houston, the singer and actress, and her business partner, Debra Chase. Their production company arranged a deal with Disney, and Houston was gearing up to portray Dandridge in a big-screen version. But Halle, believing that she was destined to play the role, bought another version of a screenplay (from A *Different World* actress

Jasmine Guy) that was based on a different Dandridge biography (written by Dandridge's manager, Earl Mills) than Houston's version. Halle approached the cable network Home Box Office and successfully pitched her project, scoring the leading role and a position as an executive producer in the process.

Which Dandridge movie would make it to the screen first? The oddsmakers were placing their bets on Halle. She was a more seasoned actress than Houston, who had only two movies to her credit at that point (1995's *Waiting to Exhale* and 1996's *The Preacher's Wife*), and Halle also bore a stronger resemblance to Dandridge than Houston did. However, fate intervened when Houston's talks with Disney were called off and she backed away from the project to pursue more viable opportunities.[29]

At long last, the Dorothy Dandridge project was now Halle's, to play her way and faithfully bring the tale of one of her role models to audiences. It would be the culmination of a lifelong dream for the actress, a crowning achievement in her career. Plans to produce the movie were well under way, and Halle cleared her schedule to devote all of her time and energy into getting it made.

NOTES

1. "Journalist Played Cupid for Couple," USA Today, May 23, 1994.

2. "Actress Halle Berry and Atlanta Braves' David Justice to Divorce," JET, March 11, 1996.

3. "Marriage Helps Justice Stay Focused," USA Today, October 11, 1993.

4. "Justice Emergency," Toronto Financial Post, June 23, 1993.

5. Edward Guthmann, " 'Losing Isaiah'—A Winner for Lange," San Francisco Chronicle," March 17, 1995.

6. Ibid.

7. Chris Hicks, "Losing Isaiah," Salt Lake City Deseret News, March 21, 1995.

8. Carrie Rickey, "Mother vs. Mother in a Battle for Son," Philadelphia Inquirer, March 17, 1995.

9. Steve Persall, "Movie on the Verge," St. Petersburg Times, March 17, 1995.

10. Joe Leydon, "The Flintstones in Viva Rock Vegas," Variety, May 17, 1994.

11. "Solid as a Rock?," Entertainment Weekly, February 18, 1994.

12. Stephen Schaefer, "Berry Mad," *EW.com*, http://www.ew.com/ew/article/0,,302549,00.html.

13. Clarence Atkins, "Halle Berry Is Enchanting as Queen of Sheba," *New York Amsterdam News*, March 4, 1995.

14. Laura B. Randolph, "Halle Berry," *Ebony*, March 1997.

15. Lisa Olson, "In the End, David Gets His Justice," *New York Daily News*, February 24, 1996.

16. Ibid.

17. "David Justice and Halle Berry Are Divorcing," *Philadelphia Inquirer*, February 24, 1996.

18. "David Justice Seeks Alimony from Estranged Wife Halle Berry," *JET*, July 29, 1996.

19. "Berry, Justice: Irreconcilable Differences," *USA Today*, May 6, 1996.

20. "David Justice Can't Give up the Halle Berry Biz," *New York Daily News*, October 5, 1997.

21. "Wit and Wisdom," *New York Daily News*, October 4, 1996.

22. Randolph, "Halle Berry."

23. Ibid.

24. Dave Kehr, " 'B.A.P.S.' Attempts to Shtick It to the Rich," *New York Daily News*, March 28, 1997.

25. Sheri Winston, "Elegant Halle Berry Plays Gritty Girl from the 'Hood B.A.P.S. Star Talks Slang and Dresses Sexy in Latest Movie," *Toronto Star*, March 25, 1997.

26. "Halle Berry Must Choose between a Black Man and White Man in TV Movie 'The Wedding,' " *JET*, February 16, 1998.

27. Tom McCarthy, *Bulworth* review, *Variety*, May 11, 1998.

28. Marjorie Baumgarten, *Bulworth* review, *Austin Chronicle*, May, 22, 1998.

29. Lucy Howard and Carla Koehl, "She's Ready for Her Close-Up," *Newsweek*, May 5, 1997.

Chapter 5

TOP OF HER GAME

A SPECIAL TELEVISION PREMIERE

Introducing Dorothy Dandridge aired for the first time on Home Box Office on August 21, 1999. It was a rewarding time for Halle Berry, who had fought relentlessly to get the movie made and spent four months filming the project, which covered Dandridge's life from her first jobs working in clubs through her tragic death.

Halle had a special connection with Dandridge for decades. It was not just that they were both born in the same Cleveland hospital—it was that Dandridge was a groundbreaking African-American actress and all-around entertainer, during a time when all of the faces on the silver screen were White and it was not enough to be just another pretty face. Dandridge spent her career struggling for acceptance and fighting for film roles, and Halle developed a tremendous amount of respect for her. No matter how difficult things would get for Halle, her adversity would pale in comparison to the hardships that Dandridge was forced to endure years before Halle even thought about a career in acting.

"I believe Dorothy passed the ball to me," Halle said. "And I say that with such strong feelings of responsibility and humility. She blazed a trail for Black actresses and fought so hard to widen horizons for our people. That's how I approach my career. I want to fight as hard as she did."[1]

Halle starred alongside actor Obba Babatundé, who played Dandridge's first husband Harold Nicholas; Brent Spiner (famous for his role as "Data" on *Star Trek: The Next Generation*, 1987–1994) as Dandridge's manager, Earl Mills; and Klaus Maria Brandauer as the notorious *Carmen Jones* (1954) director (and Dandridge love interest) Otto Preminger.

Halle was riding high on the positive reviews of the film (she would later win a Best Actress Golden Globe Award for her role) when she attended a premiere event in New York City with a slim, young soul singer she had been quietly dating named Eric Benét. The Milwaukee, Wisconsin-born Benét was part of the musical "neo-soul" movement, a group of mostly African-American singers and musicians who favored an ethnic look (natural hairstyles and beaded jewelry) and had a sound reminiscent of the rhythm-and-blues music of the 1960s and 1970s, but with an updated edge. He had released two albums, *True to Myself* in 1996 and *A Day in the Life* in 1999, and found success on the singles charts with popular songs including "Spiritual Thang," "Georgy Porgy," and "Spend My Life with You."

Halle and Benét had been dating one another since the spring of 1999, but Halle had purposefully kept mum about their relationship because she was still smarting from the publicity she had had to endure during her marriage to David Justice. The cat was out of the bag when Halle walked the red carpet hand-in-hand with Benét and looked very much in love. No one was surprised when, at year's end, the couple announced plans to marry in 2000.

AN EARLY-MORNING ACCIDENT

Things were going well for Halle both personally and professionally when she found herself at the center of a head-on car accident on February 23, 2000. She had spent the evening hanging out at the home of a female friend, by her account just having a casual, uneventful time. At around 2 a.m., Halle was driving back to her own home in a rented white Chevrolet Blazer in Los Angeles at an intersection on the Sunset Strip when she allegedly ran a red light and hit a 1996 Pontiac Sunfire. The driver of that car was Heta Raythatha, a 27-year-old real estate agent who worked as an accountant on the side and lived in nearby Santa Monica.

Halle left the scene, driving herself home despite having a gaping wound on her forehead. Halle later said she had no memory of the actual accident and did not remember leaving the scene of an accident. Later that morning, Halle collected herself and sought medical treatment at Cedars-Sinai Medical Center for her wound, which required 22 stitches,[2] and reported to police at the hospital that she had been in an accident.[3] Raythatha, who was treated for a broken right wrist at the same hospital, saw Halle but recognized her only as the movie star that everyone knew. Because she never saw who hit her, she did not know that the driver that slammed into her and the actress were one and the same. When Raythatha found out that Halle was the driver, her starstruck moment turned into rage. "She sped off and made no attempt to get me help," Raythatha complained in *InStyle* magazine. "I find everything she has told the press regarding her alleged blackout completely unbelievable."[4]

In the aftermath during the weeks that followed, Halle had to endure becoming the punch line of jokes by late-night talk-show hosts and stand-up comedians who made fun of her perceived inability to drive, and rumors spread that she had been drinking or using drugs before she had gotten behind the wheel that night. But Halle did not find any humor in the accident or the tsunami of bad publicity that followed. She was distraught by the whole experience and had difficulty eating and sleeping as she waited for the Los Angeles Superior Court to hand down its decision.

Halle was charged with a misdemeanor for the incident and pled no contest to the charge of leaving the scene of an accident. An investigation by the police revealed that she had not been speeding at the time of the crash. She was facing up to one year in jail and a $10,000 fine, but Beverly Hills Superior Court Judge Charles Rubin ended up sentencing Halle to perform 200 hours of community service and to pay a $13,500 fine. Halle was also placed on three years of probation. The driver of the other vehicle filed a separate lawsuit that accused Berry of negligence and emotional distress. Claiming that she was permanently disfigured as a result of the accident, the driver asked for unspecified damages.[5]

Halle was given the choice of how she wanted to serve the community service portion on her sentence; she chose to work at Jenesse Center, a shelter in the inner city of Los Angeles, where she worked with domestic violence survivors and their children who were trying to regain their independence and self-esteem. Halle was profoundly affected by the experience and said that she had fallen in love with everyone that she met at the shelter (Halle continues to support the shelter to this day).[6]

In the end, Halle accepted responsibility for her role in the accident and claimed to have learned some important life lessons. The issues with her father's abandonment of her as a child came back to haunt her in the accident's aftermath, and she worried that her fans would turn against her and that Benét would leave her. None of that turned out to be the case. Halle's fans rallied around her in a show of support, and Benét stayed right by her side throughout the whole ordeal. In fact, Halle credited Benét with helping her get through the difficult time and has referred to him more than once as her soul mate. The experience had brought the couple even closer together than they had ever been before, and it seemed that if they could get through the accident, they could get through anything.

OFF TO PLAY A SUPERHERO

Three weeks after the premiere of *Introducing Dorothy Dandridge*, Halle was off to film her role in *X-Men*, the movie based on the Marvel Comics series of characters created by Stan Lee, who also created Spider-Man, the Hulk, and Iron Man, among other memorable characters. The X-Men are a group of mutants who are taught by Professor Charles Xavier (also known as Professor X) to control their powers. In the film version, which was released in movie theaters in 2000, Halle played Storm, a mutant who has the ability to control the weather. Halle has said that her difficulties growing up as an interracial child help her to identify with Storm, a woman who is treated like a freak because she's different:

> It's like realizing a fantasy to play a super-heroine because the women in this movie are strong, sexy and equal to the men ... but there's much more to it than that. The mutants are outcasts of society, and being a minority I can relate to that feeling. And after the accident I felt like a freak and that nobody could understand.[7]

The movie was a huge success—not just with hard-core comic book fans, but with the general public as well. " 'X-Men' is a distinctively absorbing entertainment, offering just enough popcorn thrills for mass audiences and just enough chewiness for hardcore sci-fi fans," said Salon.com.[8] It became Halle's highest-grossing film to date, raking in over $54 million during its opening weekend and earning $242 million worldwide.

A SECRET WEDDING

The entertainment press and Halle's dedicated fans eagerly awaited the announcement of Halle and Benét's marriage, but as the year passed, it seemed the couple was going to stay engaged much longer than they had planned. As it turned out, the twosome had pulled a fast one: they had made their union official at a secret wedding sometime in January 2001 in Los Angeles. It truly was a private affair—no one has ever confirmed who was on the guest list—it is unknown if there were even any witnesses at all—and no pictures of the nuptials have even been released to members of the press.

Three months after their nuptials, Halle and Eric sued the tabloid magazine *Star* for $5 million when it printed a story that their marriage was on the rocks.[9]

Despite the negative stories in the press, Halle dove into her new roles as a wife to Benét and as stepmother to his daughter, India, who was nine years old at the time. India's mother, Tami Marie Stauff, was killed in a car accident when India was still a baby, and Benét had been raising her on his own until Halle came into his life. Halle and India quickly formed a tight bond, and Halle devoted herself to being a constant maternal presence in the young girl's life. The two were frequently spotted in Los Angeles shopping together, and Halle even skipped the premiere of the movie *Ali* (2001, which starred Will Smith in an Oscar-nominated performance) to help India rehearse her lines and work on her costume for a school play.[10]

THE ROLE OF A LIFETIME

Halle had found some creative freedom in the roles that she had done for the small screen, and that same spirit is what attracted her to a big part in a low-budget, independent film that some considered to be beneath an artist of her stature.

Monster's Ball (2001) was the pet project of Marc Forster, a maverick young director. The film's title is taken from a medieval reference to the circumstances and events surrounding a prisoner before his execution. Halle played Leticia Musgrove, the wife of Lawrence, an inmate on death row (played by Sean "Puffy" Combs) with a talent for drawing. Early in the film, Leticia says goodbye to her husband before he is executed. The movie follows Leticia as she struggles to survive and deal with her grief while trying to raise her son, who struggles with his weight and hoards the food he eats for comfort.

Forster had auditioned several actresses for the role (including, reportedly, Queen Latifah) and did not want to give the part to Halle at first. But, as she had done many times before, she fought for it, proving in the end that she was not too glamorous or too fragile to play Leticia. "I just wore him down," Halle said. "I shared with him some moments in my life. Some were personal moments of heartbreak, hard knocks. I can relate to Leticia in ways that you wouldn't think I can if you're just looking at me."[11]

Hank Grotowski (Billy Bob Thornton, an Oscar winner for his role in the 1996 film *Sling Blade*) works at the local prison with his son, Sonny (Heath Ledger), and develops a bond with Leticia's husband before he escorts him to his death. Hank has demons of his own: he is forced to share his home with his ailing, racist father (Peter Boyle) and struggles with the bitter disappointment he feels toward his son, who throws up during Lawrence's execution and is seen as a weak loser in Hank's eyes.

Hank and Leticia meet and are drawn together in their shared misery; they embark on a romance as they both endure additional tragedies throughout the film. "A heart-wrenching but rewarding experience, as well as a showcase for some of the best acting you'll see this season," wrote Jack Garner for Gannett News Service.[12] "Berry—playing against type in the performance to beat among actresses this year—is volcanic," said Peter Travers in a review for *Rolling Stone* magazine.[13]

One notorious scene featured an explicit sexual encounter between Leticia and Hank. Much was made of the scene in the press, with most of the attention focusing on Halle's decision to appear nude. In previous films, Halle had refused to bare all. But Halle thought that the scene was important enough to the storyline to relax her conservative stance. "I call that scene the kiss of life, from that moment the choices these characters made affected their lives and it made them able to have a better life," she said.[14]

To prepare for the role, Halle worked with Ivana Chubbuck, an acting coach from Michigan who has worked with several Hollywood heavyweights (including Jon Voight, Brad Pitt, Jim Carrey, and Sharon Stone). "She wasn't an actor's actor when she came to me," Chubbuck said. "I changed her life in that respect."[15]

Director Forster had to cut plenty of corners to get the movie made and recalled that Halle never once acted like a diva that was doing him a favor by agreeing to appear in his independent film. Halle never made the crew wait for her to come onto the set, and she gave gifts to all of the members of the crew when the movie wrapped production. When *Monster's Ball* was screened at the Berlin International Film Festival, Halle stopped by a dinner that Forster was hosting for friends and quietly picked up the tab when she had to leave early. "That's Halle," Forster said admiringly.[16]

Released on February 8, 2001, *Monster's Ball* was like the little film that could. Made for an estimated $4 million, it started out slow, released in a small number of national theaters, but the controversy, word of mouth, and positive reviews attracted moviegoers and it went on to gross $20 million at the box office.

Halle later said that making *Monster's Ball* was cathartic and that watching it for the first time was emotionally draining. She also stated that it was the first time she was able to watch a movie that she had been in and disconnect herself from the character she was portraying.[17]

A NEGATIVE RESPONSE TO *MONSTER'S BALL*

However, there was a bit of backlash in the African-American community regarding Halle's role. Some felt the part was exploitive for portraying a poor, Black woman as abusive and sexually vulnerable to the advances of a White man in a position of power.

Depictions of African-American women having sex on-screen were rare at the time the movie was released. In fact, if a Black woman was seen having sex on-screen at all, it was usually with a Black male actor in a movie aimed at a predominately Black audience, such as the Blaxploitation films of the 1970s (*Shaft*, 1971, *Foxy Brown*, 1974, and *Super Fly*, 1972) and the movies of Spike Lee (director of Halle's debut film *Jungle Fever*, 1971, as well as *She's Gotta Have It*, 1986, and *Mo' Better Blues*, 1990). It was rarer still to see a White man depicted as the sexual partner of a Black female. Even movies such as *Guess Who's Coming to Dinner* (1967) that featured an interracial couple sidestepped around portrayals of sexual relations.

The issue that many people seemed to have with this particular sex scene—which is indeed much rawer and more explicit than most sex scenes seen in mainstream cinema—in *Monster's Ball* was that they felt that it was pornographic and beneath an actress of Halle's caliber. Halle and Thornton do appear nude in the scene, and the sexual act is more animalistic than romantic. It was rumored that *Monster's Ball* nearly earned an "X" rating from the Motion Picture Association of America because the scene was too sexually explicit. The scene was trimmed to allow it to be shown in more theaters, as an "X" rating would have kept it out of the majority of movie theaters in the country. Still, rumors circulated that the two actors were really having sex in the scenes, which added fuel to the controversy.

Many of the most vehement critics felt that the sex scene between Halle and Thornton was too graphic, including Angela Bassett, the African-American actress best known for her Academy Award–nominated role as Tina Turner in the film biography *What's Love Got to Do with It?* (1993). In an interview, Bassett reportedly claimed that she had been offered the role but turned it down because she thought it would make her look like a prostitute on film or perpetuate what she felt was a stereotypical depiction of an African-American woman.[18]

Film producer Stanley Tatum (*The Laramie Project*, 2002, and *A Beautiful Mind*, 2001) voiced his strong opinion of *Monster's Ball* and his frustration with portrayals of race in the movies. "It's amazing the vacuum black people exist in cinematically, having no options, let alone a developed character. So the white character [referring to Thornton's role in *Monster's Ball*] can come in like Sir Galahad, giving the downtrodden Negress a lifeline." To Halle's credit, Tatum did add that her performance "rose above the material and the subject matter."[19]

Miles Willis, the African-American activist and host of *Milestones*, a jazz radio program that aired on station KPFT in Houston, Texas, was one of several prominent people who urged a boycott of *Monster's Ball*, writing, "Imagine the seething indignation that a Jewish man might feel while watching a story in which the widow of a Nazi concentration camp victim has an intimate relationship with the SS officer that shoved her husband into one of those ovens at Auschwitz!"[20]

An organized protest of the movie failed to come together, and a petition that circulated via the Internet calling for a boycott of Lions Gate Entertainment Corporation and of Halle's films fizzled. The controversy died down temporarily shortly after the movie was released in theaters.

Bassett's and Willis's opinions, however, were derided by dozens of prominent movie critics who felt Halle's performance was groundbreaking and applauded her bravery.[21]

> Halle Berry is a revelation as the woman who opens Thornton's heart. She's tried to shed a sexpot image in earlier films, but this is by far her most electrifying work to date. She disappears into the character of an ignorant, helpless woman and tears at our emotions without ever begging for sympathy,[22]

wrote Movieline's Stephen Farber. "Ms. Berry pours heart and soul into her performance in a role that demands vulnerability far beyond mere naked skin. From the brink of oblivion, Leticia drags herself back to life, and it is an astonishing feat to watch," opined the Cincinnati Enquirer's Margaret A. McGurk.[23] The forward momentum of Halle's career continued despite the protests of her detractors.

A MEATIER ACTION ROLE

Halle's next appearance on-screen would be in Swordfish (2001), a counterespionage action thriller featuring a cast led by John Travolta (Saturday Night Fever, 1977, Pulp Fiction, 1994, and The Taking of Pelham 1-2-3, 2009). Travolta played Gabriel, a wealthy criminal who sends his associate, Ginger (played by Halle Berry), to hire the services of a Stanley Jobson (Halle's X-Men costar Hugh Jackman), a computer genius who accepts $10 million from Gabriel to write a program that will allow him to steal money from a government slush fund. Actor Don Cheadle (Ocean's Eleven, 2001, and Hotel Rwanda, 2004) also starred in the film as an FBI agent keeping tabs on Stanley.

The movie was notable for its impressive, eye-popping opening sequence, during which a human hostage bomb detonates in spectacular fashion. The rest of the movie unfolds in complicated twists and turns, but was notable for its jam-packed action sequences and special effects, including a recreation of the stunning slow-motion bullet scene best remembered from the futuristic 1999 action film *The Matrix*.

Once again, this film would be notable for Halle's decision to go bare—this time, it was for a topless scene that did not exactly appear to be integral to the movie's plot. In the scene, Halle's character is lounging reading a book, which she drops to casually reveal that her breasts are exposed. Rumors spread that Halle had asked for additional compensation to disrobe, a figure that was quoted as somewhere been $400,000 all the way up to $1 million. Both Halle and the film's producers denied that this was true, but the buzz and the controversy created certainly did not hurt it at the box office. Released in June, *Swordfish* appealed to a much wider audience than *Monster's Ball* and pulled in $70 million in ticket sales. "Ruthlessly grabbing your attention from the very beginning, Swordfish kick starts with a jaw-dropping spectacle of mass carnage that is one of the most impressive scenes of utter destruction in cinematic history to date," wrote Radio Free critic Andrew Manning.[24]

HALLE'S EDGY ROLE MAKES CINEMATIC HISTORY

Prior to the 2002 Academy Awards, only four African-Americans had received best acting honors: Hattie McDaniel was the first, winning Best Supporting Actress for her role in *Gone with the Wind* in 1939. Nearly four decades would pass before another African-American would win—Louis Gossett, Jr., who received the Best Supporting Actor nod in 1983 for his portrayal of a tough military boot camp instructor in "*An Officer and a Gentleman*" (1982). In 1991, comedienne and actress Whoopi Goldberg took a Best Supporting Actress award home for her role as a clairvoyant in *Ghost* (1990); six years later, Cuba Gooding, Jr.'s work playing an enigmatic football player in *Jerry Maguire* (1996) earned him 1997 Best Supporting Actor honors.

Monster's Ball racked up nominations for several prestigious awards, and Halle went on to win several Best Actress nods for her performance, including the Screen Actor's Guild Award, the National Board of Review of Motion Pictures Award, and the Berlin International Film Festival Award. So it was no surprise when, on February 12, 2002, the nominations for the Academy Awards were announced and Halle was listed among the contenders in the Best Actress category.

Halle attended the traditional pre-awards Nominees Luncheon at the Beverly Hilton Hotel on March 11. She took her rightful place among the other 103 nominees who attended in a group photo that commemorated the event. Wearing a sleek grey skirt suit, Halle was beaming as she posed for photos with Denzel Washington, Will Smith, and the other stars, directors, writers, and other honored guests who shared the honor of being nominated.

The 74th annual Academy Awards ceremony was held on March 24, 2002. It was slightly windy, but the sun was shining—a good omen. The festivities took place at the brand new Kodak Theater, which is located at the corner of Hollywood Boulevard and North Highland Avenue in downtown Los Angeles. Whoopi Goldberg (cohost, ABC's *The View*) served as host of the Oscars ceremony for the fourth time. The show would clock in at 4 hours and 23 minutes, making it the longest Oscar show to date.

The event was a lavish affair, and everyone who was anyone in Hollywood walked the red carpet past crowds of screaming fans and hundreds of members of the paparazzi to take their seats inside the theater. Halle, wearing a breathtaking brown Elie Saab gown with a sheer top embroidered with flowers and leaves, sat between her mother, Judith, and her husband, Eric Benét.

Goldberg entertained the crowd and the millions of people watching the broadcast worldwide with her elaborate production numbers and hilarious jokes, and the celebrated acrobatic circus troupe Cirque du Soleil wowed the crowd with its breathtaking artistry. The Academy Award ceremony was notable for several contested awards: in the Best Actor category, Will Smith (nominated for playing the title role in the Muhammad Ali biopic *Ali*, 2001) was up against Denzel Washington for his part as a crooked cop in the action drama *Training Day* (2001—Washington would win the award); Sidney Poitier, the legendary African-American actor (*To Sir, With Love*, 1967, and *Guess Who's Coming to Dinner?*, 1967) received an honorary Oscar, as did acclaimed actor and director Robert Redford (*Butch Cassidy and the Sundance Kid*, 1969, and *Indecent Proposal*, 1993).

The Best Picture category was difficult to predict, with *In the Bedroom*, *Gosford Park*, *Moulin Rouge!*, *The Lord of the Rings: The Fellowship of the Rings*, and *A Beautiful Mind* (the eventual winner) in the running.

In the Best Actress category, Halle's competition was Dame Judi Dench for *Iris* (a biopic about the novelist Iris Murdoch), Nicole Kidman for the Baz Luhrmann–directed musical *Moulin Rouge!*, Sissy Spacek for the tear-jeaking tragic drama *In the Bedroom*, and Renée Zellweger for the romantic comedy/chick flick *Bridget Jones's Diary*. Formidable opponents all, and while there was no clear frontrunner, Halle was seen as a viable contender thanks to the other awards she had received earlier that year. But Halle, who respected the work of her competitors and felt that they had all turned in strong performances, did not really think that she had a chance. She was so convinced that she would not win the award that she did not prepare an acceptance speech beforehand and planned to just enjoy the evening and revel in the significance of her nomination.

Australian actor Russell Crowe, who had won the Best Actor Oscar the year before for the epic *Gladiator* (2002) and was nominated again that night for his leading role in *A Beautiful Mind* (which would take home Best Picture and Best Director honors) read the list of Best Actress nominees before the winner's name would be read. After he tore open the envelope, he announced Halle's name as the winner, and Halle looked as though she was genuinely shocked to have won. In the broadcast, Halle was seen saying "Oh my God!" over and over as she was congratulated by all of the people sitting around her. She gave her mother a hug before she stood up, hugged her husband, and walked up to the stage. Russell Crowe gave Halle a congratulatory hug and patted her on the back before handing her the statuette (it was revealed later that Crowe told the hyperventilating Halle to "breathe"[25]).

"Oh my God," Halle repeated at the microphone, and as she struggled to collect her emotions, her husband rose to his feet again to lead another round of applause. Halle's comments came off the top of her head; her extemporaneous speech lasted three minutes. "This moment is so much bigger than me," she said. "This moment is for Dorothy Dandridge, Lena Horne, Diahann Carroll . . . it's for the women that stand beside me: Jada Pinkett, Angela Bassett, Viveca Fox

... and it's for every nameless, faceless woman of color that now has a chance, because this door tonight has been opened." After more applause, Halle continued,

I'm so honored, and I thank the Academy for choosing me to be the vessel from which this blessing might flow, thank you . . . I want to thank my manager, Vincent Cirrincione . . . I want to thank my mom, who's given me the strength to fight every single day to be who I want to be and gave me the courage to dream that this dream might be happening and possible for me, I love you mom, so much, thank you. My husband, who is just the joy of my life, and India, thank you for giving me peace, because only with the peace that you've brought me have I been allowed to go to places that I never even knew I could go . . . thank you, I love you and India with all my heart.[26]

Halle went on to thank several more of the influential people in her personal and professional life, including *Monster's Ball* director Marc Forster and producer Lee Daniels; her acting coach, Ivana Chubbuck; her lawyer, Neil Myer; director Spike Lee, for casting her in her first film (*Jungle Fever*, 1991); and Oprah Winfrey, for being a role model. When Halle left the stage, she was teary-eyed and triumphant.

While the reality of what she had accomplished would not truly sink in for several days, Halle was flying high. After decades of struggling to be accepted by her peers, she had finally made it all the way to the top and been awarded the most prestigious honor that an actor can ever receive. All of her life, Halle had dreamed that her Oscar-winning moment was possible, and even though she had been knocked down several times on her way to the top, she had finally done it. Halle Berry had officially arrived.

After Halle left the stage with her Oscar statuette (like all of the rest of the winners, she would have to give the award back so that her name could be engraved on it later) firmly in hand, she was whisked into the media room of the theater where she spent five minutes being photographed with her trophy by dozens of photographers and then was escorted into another room where she fielded questions from the press and apologized for failing to thank Thornton, her *Monster's Ball* costar, in her speech. Then, finally, she was reunited with her mother and husband and was off to celebrate.

WHATEVER HAPPENED TO HALLE'S FATHER?

The part of Halle's Oscar speech in which she referred to her manager as the only father she had ever known piqued the media's interest about her real father. Where was he at this high point in his estranged daughter's life, and where had he been since he had abandoned his wife and daughters all of those years ago? Jerome Berry was finally located at the Indian Hills Health & Rehabilitation Center in Cleveland, where he was allegedly living off of his government benefits and was suffering from the effects of Parkinson's disease, a disorder that affects the central nervous system and results in impaired speech and physical functioning.

According to an article published in the *Mirror* (London), Jerome's ability to speak had deteriorated to the point that he was unable to talk, but Renee Berry Graves, a woman living in Montgomery, Alabama, who claimed to be one of Jerome's daughters and, therefore, Halle's half sister, made a plea to Halle through the media to reach out to her father and forgive him for his past wrongdoings. Halle, for her part, has said that while she has indeed forgiven her father for the years of abuse and abandonment, she cannot forget the past and considered him to be a stranger.[27] She would not reach out to Jerome Berry, and there is no record or acknowledgment on Halle's part that she spoke to or met with him at this time in her life.

BECOMING A BOND GIRL

Halle would make history yet again for another groundbreaking performance. *Die Another Day* (2002) was the 20th installment in the James Bond series of movies, which were based on 12 different novels and 2 short stories by author Ian Fleming. James Bond is a dashing member of the British Secret Intelligence Service who uses his skills to diffuse the efforts of criminals and terrorists and finds the time to romance some of the world's most beautiful women.

Throughout the years, several different actors have portrayed James Bond on film. Sean Connery was the first, in 1962's *Dr. No*, and would reprise his role in five other Bond movies. Actor George Lazenby took one turn as Bond in *On Her Majesty's Secret Service* in 1969. He was succeeded by Roger Moore, who started his run in 1973's *Live and Let Die* and starred in six others, including *Moonraker* (1979) and

A View to a Kill (1985). Timothy Dalton played Bond twice, in 1987's *The Living Daylights* and 1989's *License to Kill*, before handing the reigns over to Pierce Brosnan. Brosnan had taken three turns at playing the suave international spy (*GoldenEye*, 1995, *Tomorrow Never Dies*, 1997, and *The World Is Not Enough*, 1999) before it was announced that he would reprise the role yet again in 2002's *Die Another Day*.

In the plot of *Die Another Day*, James Bond thinks that he has killed a rogue North Korean colonel and is captured and tortured. After he is released in a prisoner exchange, Bond discovers that it was someone inside his own organization that leaked his whereabouts and was responsible for his capture. Bond sets out to find the source of the leak while attempting to prevent a satellite from starting a war between rivals North and South Korea.

During a trip to Cuba, Bond meets Jinx (Halle Berry), who makes a memorable entrance in the film by emerging from the coastal waters in an orange bikini accessorized by a silver dagger strapped to her thigh. Jinx helps Bond find the colonel he thought he killed and reappears again in Iceland when Bond infiltrates the ice palace of British billionaire Gustav Graves, who is somehow connected to the colonel. During the course of the movie, Bond and Jinx have a torrid affair and Bond saves her from drowning.

As Jinx, Halle joined the elite ranks of the other "Bond Girls," a series of female characters elevated to cult status for their prominent roles as sassy, tough, and yes, sexy love interests in the Bond films. Other memorable Bond girls include Honey Ryder (played by Ursula Andress in 1962's *Dr. No*, Pussy Galore (portrayed by Honor Blackman in 1964's *Goldfinger*), and, of course, Octopussy, played by actress Maud Adams in the 1983 film of the same name. The role of a Bond Girl is one of the most coveted, high-profile jobs for any actress to get—and as an African-American woman, Halle became a member of an even more exclusive club. Actress Gloria Hendry was the first African-American Bond Girl (in *Live and Let Die*) and Grace Jones in *A View to a Kill* was the second. Halle Berry had the honor of becoming the third.

While filming one of their love scenes, Halle famously choked on a piece of fruit. A quick-thinking Brosnan leapt to action and performed the Heimlich maneuver to help Halle dislodge the food and clear her windpipe so she could breathe again. She was also injured on the set in Cádiz, Spain, when a smoke grenade used for special effects went off and pieces of it flew into her eye, causing it to become inflamed. A 30-minute operation removed the particles, and Halle was given a clean bill of health and allowed to continue filming.

Die Another Day opened in November 2002 to mostly lackluster reviews. "Dissing a Bond movie is quite like calling a dog stupid ... the dialogue is pablum ... the plot idiotic," wrote a critic in the *New York Village Voice*.[28] "Jinx is fun. Jinx is hot. But Jinx will still have to be rescued by her man in the apocalyptic final reel of this overlong, two-plus hour destruction derby," wrote another critic in the *Montreal Gazette*.[29] but their thoughts did nothing to keep movie fans away. "Die Another Day" was a worldwide box-office success, earning $425 million in ticket sales.

Revlon, the cosmetics company for which Halle had been a spokes-model, launched a limited-edition 007 makeup collection to coincide with the release of *Die Another Day*. Dubbed "The Look of Jinx," the blush, mascara, lipstick, and nail polish were available for a limited time in select drugstores.

The movie *Die Another Day* had done so well that there was talk of a spin-off movie that would focus on Jinx, with Halle reprising the role. The movie was in development with MGM Studios and looked as though it would become a reality, but the project was canceled a year later.

PLANNING FOR CHILDREN DESPITE PROBLEMS

The day after *Die Another Day* opened in theaters, Halle announced that she would take time off to focus on her personal life and attempt to get pregnant. At 34, Halle felt that she was growing older and was concerned about her fertility. While she enjoyed being an involved stepmother to Benét's then 12-year-old daughter India—and even formally adopted the girl so that she would legally become her daughter—Halle had always wanted to have a child of her own. She said that she did not want to miss her chance. She had planned to take three months off around the Christmas holiday to devote all of her energy to conceiving.

Shortly after her announcement it was revealed that Halle and Benét were having marriage troubles. Halle chose not to deny the rumors, but refused to confirm that Benét had had numerous extramarital affairs with other women and had been treated at The Meadows, a clinic in Arizona, for sexual addiction. Halle later revealed in an interview with Oprah that she had found out that Benét had an affair 10 days after her Oscar win, and she was on the set of *Die Another Day* when she had learned that he had had more than one affair. Halle said she had suffered an emotional breakdown as a result and even contemplated suicide for a second time.[30]

The alleged woman who had had the most recent affair with Benét was Julia Riley, a 33-year-old model. Riley sold her story to the tabloids, claiming that she had slept with Benét days before Halle won her Academy Award. Benét was supposedly photographed by paparazzi leaving Riley's apartment in Milwaukee, Wisconsin, and Riley told a reporter that Benét had sent her text messages telling her that he loved her.[31]

At her mother Judith's suggestion, Halle went with Benét to see a marital counselor to attempt to repair their shattered relationship. Halle's heart was broken, but she was determined to stand by her man, choosing to view his sexual addiction in the same light as one would an addiction to drugs or alcohol. Benét professed that he was still in love his wife and that he, too, wanted to save their marriage. Halle was sure that he could overcome his issues and that they would be stronger for having made it through the ordeal.

THE DEATH OF HALLE'S LONG-LOST FATHER

On January 24, 2003, Halle's father, Jerome, died at the Indian Hills Health & Rehabilitation Center in Cleveland. He had been suffering from the effects of Parkinson's disease, a degenerative brain disorder that affects memory and the ability to function independently. Halle released no comment about the man who had been abusive to her mother and sister and abandoned their family when she was still a young girl. Reportedly, Halle had not seen or spoken to him at all in the years that followed.

Halle's older half sister, Renee Berry Graves, attempted to reach out to Halle via the press before Jerome died to repair their fractured relationship, but Halle declined to make contact. In the years that followed, Halle has spoken very little about her father and the influence that his abuse and absence had on her life and relationships with men.

A SURPRISE SMOOCH

It is a tradition that the winner of the Best Actress category present the award to the following year's Best Actor winner, and 2003 was no exception. Halle graciously returned to the stage of the Kodak Theater to read the list of nominated actors and their 2002 movies: Nicolas Cage for *Adaptation*, Jack Nicholson for *About Schmidt*, Daniel Day-Lewis for "*Gangs of New York*," Michael Caine for *The Quiet American*, and Adrien Brody for *The Pianist*.

Halle announced Brody's name as the winner, and the excited 29-year-old (the youngest Best Actor winner in the history of the Awards) bounded up to the stage to claim his statuette. Caught up in the moment, Brody swept Halle into his arms and kissed her on the mouth, dipping her back dramatically as he did so. Halle was taken completely by surprise. Her mouth hung open in shock, but she quickly recovered and stepped aside. "I bet they didn't tell you that was in the gift bag," Brody said to Halle before launching into the rest of his acceptance speech.

X-MEN, PART 2

X-Men (2000) was such a runaway success that demands for a sequel were made, and all of the original characters from the first movie were reunited for the second. The plot of *X2: X-Men United* (2003) picked up several months after the original ended. The X-Men had success-fully captured rogue mutant Magneto and imprisoned him, but his partner, Mystique, has managed to break him out of his plastic cell. Now, the X-Men have to find a way to stop Magneto from organizing the other mutants to support his evil schemes, deal with increasing tensions between mutants and humans, and rescue Professor X.

Halle appeared again as the weather-controlling Storm. While she is in the center of some visually impressive special effects, her screen time is minimal compared to that of the other characters.

Premiering in April 2003, *X-Men* ruled at the box office, making a staggering $406 million worldwide. The door was left open yet again for the possibility of another installment.

"*X-Men 2* is a blaze of special effects, high-octane action scenes and quirky characters," wrote *Sunday Mail* critic Paul Kermode. "It all adds up to an enjoyable romp."[32]

Halle was reportedly unhappy with the lack of screen time that she had and wished that the writers and producers would have given her character the depth and presence that Storm had in the X-Men comic books.

END OF A UNION

In October 2003, Halle's marriage to Benét had finally run its course, and she announced that they were separating. "Eric and I have had marital problems for some time now and have tried to work things out together," Halle said in a prepared statement.[33] Six months later, she formally filed for divorce from Benét, citing irreconcilable differences.

Benét was quick to challenge their prenuptial agreement and filed court papers to determine if they were valid and enforceable. He also wanted Halle to pay his legal bills and sought spousal support.[34] In a television interview, Benét denied the charges of sexual addiction but admitted that he had made "some really, really stupid, painful mistakes" and that he had engaged in verbally inappropriate behavior and inappropriate physical contact. He also admitted that he had had difficulty standing in his superstar wife's shadow and that his ego took a blow when the media constantly referred to him as "Mr. Halle Berry."[35]

Halle was once again disappointed by a failed marriage, but said that she would not let the lack of a spouse keep her from having the children she knew that she still wanted to have someday. "I'll adopt," she said. "I'll get artificially inseminated. "I'll do whatever I will have to do. I really don't want to miss motherhood in my life, and I know I love children."[36]

Two years later, Benét released his first album in six years (Hurricane) on which he said several of the soul-tinged songs were inspired by the breakup of his marriage. He claimed that he had learned from the ordeal and emerged as a new person.[37] The album received some critical acclaim but was poorly received by the record-buying public.

TWO STALKERS DENIED

Many Hollywood celebrities have been stalked by rabid, delusional fans, and, starting in 2004, Halle Berry was no exception. Greg Broussard, a Louisiana native, had attempted several times to contact Halle by phone and fax and believed that he and Halle were in a relationship and that they were engaged to be married. He alleged that Halle's staff was keeping Halle away from him. Halle asserted that she had never heard of Broussard—and certainly did not have a relationship with him—and feared for her safety. Broussard was ordered by a court in Santa Monica, California, to stay 100 yards away from Halle, her manager, Vincent Cirrincione, and her publicist, Karen Samfilippo.

Less than a year later, Robert Sawyer of San Paulo, California, repeatedly sent Halle dozens of letters professing his love and delusions of a romantic relationship. Halle's security team contacted Sawyer and asked him to stop trying to contact Halle, but Sawyer continued, even telling her in one of his letters that he was planning a Valentine's Day visit to fulfill their relationship. Sawyer attempted to claim that the whole incident was the result of mistaken identity and possible fraud and asked for forgiveness. He wrote in documents that were submitted to the court that his contacts with the real Halle Berry started after he met a woman who called herself Halle and asked him to write a manuscript for her. Halle did not buy his story and filed a lawsuit. A judge issued a three-year restraining order and ordered Sawyer to stay 100 yards away from Halle, her home, work, and vehicle.

A SCARY THRILLER

The end of 2003 marked the release of *Gothika*, a suspense thriller in which Halle costarred with Robert Downey, Jr. (*Less Than Zero*, 1987, and *Ironman*, 2008). Halle was paid $6 million for her role.[38]

In *Gothika*, Halle played the role of Miranda Grey, a repressed psychiatrist who mysteriously wakes up one day as a patient in the mental institution where she works. Miranda has been accused of murdering her husband, but she has no memory of the events that supposedly took place and is being haunted by a ghost named Rachel. Downey plays Pete Graham, a colleague of Grey's who is keeping her locked up despite his romantic feelings for her.

During the filming of the movie the year before in Montreal, Halle broke her arm—specifically, the ulna, a bone in her arm—during a physical scene (no stunts were being filmed at the time). She was forced to wear a plaster cast below her elbow, and production was halted for a week as the producers of the film tried to find a way to shoot around the cast. Benét flew in from Los Angeles and rushed to the set to be by Halle's side and help her recuperate.

Filming resumed and *Gothika* wrapped in time for a November release. "Berry can act, all right, but she can also simply evoke, and here, where she's required to fight her way out of a nightmare, that quality is crucial," wrote film critic Roger Ebert in his review of the movie. "She carries us along with her, while logic and plausibility simply become irrelevant."[39]

The scary movie made just over $19 million during its opening weekend and grossed $59.6 million in the United States. Fred Durst, a White rock singer who was the former front man for the popular rock band Limp Bizkit ("Nookie"), sang a song on the movie's soundtrack, "Behind Blue Eyes," and Halle appeared in the music video. A scene in which Halle kisses Durst sparked rumors that the two were romantically involved—a story that Durst played coy about in the press but Halle emphatically denied.

THE PUBLIC FACE OF A DISEASE

Halle had been diagnosed with a form of diabetes while in her early 20s after she had unexpectedly fallen into a diabetic coma while filming the television series *Living Dolls*; since then she had managed to keep her condition under control through diet, exercise, insulin therapy, and careful monitoring of her blood sugar levels.

While she had mentioned her condition in interviews over the years and served as an active volunteer for the Juvenile Diabetes Association, she had not come out as an official spokesperson for diabetes until she was approached by Novo Nordisk, a pharmaceutical company that creates products to help diabetics manage their conditions. Nordisk asked Halle to become the first national ambassador for its "Diabetes Aware" campaign in 2004. A partnership with the Entertainment Industry Foundation, Diabetes Aware was a public health initiative designed to educate Americans about the importance of diabetes detection, monitoring, and proper management of diabetes, which is a chronic and progressive disease. The campaign encouraged people to get a simple blood glucose test to determine if they have the disease—as many as 20 million people living in America live with diabetes, but only half of them are even aware that they have the disease and could become sick or even die without the proper treatment and medical care. Halle appeared in print ads and is still prominently featured on the Diabetes Aware Web site (www.diabetesaware.com) as part of the ongoing effort to raise awareness of the disease.

AN IM-PURRFECT ROLE AS A CARTOON CRIME FIGHTER

From the start, *Catwoman* sounded like the perfect star vehicle for Halle. The movie was based on the female antiheroine from "Batman," the legendary caped crusader first popularized in the DC Comics. The character of Catwoman was first introduced in 1940, when she was the alter ego of Selina Kyle and was known simply as "The Cat." Known for her catsuit and mask (complete with cat-like ears and a long tail), her skills with a whip, and her penchant for stealing, The Cat became Catwoman over the years and was portrayed in the 1960s television series by White actresses Julie Newmar and Lee Meriwether (a former Miss America) and also by African-American singer/chanteuse Eartha Kitt. In the 1992 film *Batman Returns*, Michelle Pfeiffer played Catwoman, starring opposite Michael Keaton as Batman and Danny DeVito as the Penguin.

In 2004, it would be Halle's turn. Some Hollywood insiders thought that the project was beneath her—now that she had won an Oscar for her acting, it was believed that playing the lead in a movie based on a comic book character would be a step backward in her efforts to be seen as a serious actress. It was a risky choice, a definite gamble, but the appeal of the role was too hard for Halle to pass up: an African-American woman had never been offered such a role as "Catwoman" before, and Halle already had a taste of how popular a comic book movie could be when she starred in *X-Men* and *X-Men 2*. This time, she would be the star, not part of a large ensemble cast. "We decided to green light her in 'Catwoman' based on her performance in which she won an Academy Award, and because we thought she was right for the role," said Jeff Robinov, president for production at Warner Bros. Studios.[40] To sweeten the deal, Halle was paid $14 million— her highest payday ever. With *Catwoman*, Halle soared into the top of the list of Hollywood's highest-paid actresses—a small and exclusive club that counts Julia Roberts, Nicole Kidman, Reese Witherspoon, Cameron Diaz, and Angelina Jolie among its members. If *Catwoman* was the success that every one associated with it was hoping it would be, Halle would become a bona fide superstar, an undeniable, influential force in the industry.

Pitof, a Frenchman known for his work on the edgy and visually dazzling foreign films *Delicatessen* (1991) and *The City of Lost Children* (1995), was chosen to direct the film. The screenplay and story of "Catwoman" were crafted by the writing duo John Brancato and Michael Ferris, who had previously worked together on *Terminator 3: The Rise of the Machines* (2003) and *The Net* (1995), which starred Sandra Bullock.

The Brancato and Ferris screenplay created a new alter ego for Catwoman: that of Patience Phillips, a meek and quiet young woman who works as a graphic designer at a large cosmetics company. One morning, she decides to rescue a cat on her windowsill and climbs out to get it, nearly falling to her death in the process. Tom Lone (Benjamin Bratt), a detective, spots her and thinks she is trying to kill herself. He saves her, and they eventually start to date one another.

During a late night at work, Patience accidentally overhears a conversation between her boss, George Hedare (Lambert Wilson) and his wife, Laurel (Sharon Stone) about a youth-restoring cream that is being rushed to market—despite long-term research that proves that the wonder cosmetic will eventually and irreversibly decay skin. Patience is spotted, and she is chased into a water tunnel and drowns. An Egyptian Mau cat brings her back to life, and Patience becomes the Catwoman, a supernatural being with cat-like reflexes, agility, and heightened senses. As Catwoman, Patience sets out to get her revenge, but is set up for the murder of the scientist who created the cream. Catwoman attempts to clear her name while Patience juggles her relationship with Detective Lone and attempts to throw him off of Catwoman's scent.

Much of the buzz surrounding the movie centered around Halle's costume: a skintight, belly-baring black leather bodysuit accentuated by a sexy bra top and strategically placed "cat scratch" rips up and down the legs. The outfit did much to highlight Halle's lean, curvy physique and guaranteed that more than a few men would turn up just to see it on the film's opening weekend.

Second to Halle's revealing costume in the movie's buzz were the special effects. Pitof spared no expense, creating computer-generated images (CGI) that brought the character's physical prowess and other-worldly abilities to the next level. Indeed, the CGI scenes of Catwoman leaping from rooftop to rooftop and propelling herself through the air were some of the slickest effects ever done in a motion picture, and previews for the film offered a teasing glimpse of what the audience would have in store.

Filming went smoothly for the most part, but Halle did suffer an injury during an action scene that required her to run at a breakneck pace. Halle did as the scene required, but she managed to run right into a piece of set equipment in the process. She was treated overnight for a minor injury and was released from the hospital the following day.

The biggest test of Halle's career, *Catwoman* opened in theaters in July 2004. Expectations were high for the dark, campy thriller, but the movie was swiftly slammed by critics and shunned by moviegoers. Reel.com gave *Catwoman* two out of four stars in one of the kinder reviews of the film and praised Halle's performance:

> Berry does a wonderful job with all three versions of her character: Patience, Catwoman, and a woman utterly confused by the havoc she's wreaking on her own life. The havoc is long-overdue, though, and as Catwoman investigates Patience's death—it's neither clear nor germane whether the death is symbolic or literal—her human side gains confidence.[41]

For most movie reviewers, it was open season, and they sharpened their claws and held nothing back in their critiques. "Much like a cat, the movie is a superfluous gob of fluff with an attitude ranging from idiotic to nasty," said the *Dallas Observer*.[42] "Berry is giving a performance much too earnest to have been intentionally campy, setting herself up as a veritable shoo-in for this year's 'Worst Actress' Razzie. Me-ouch!" said *Premiere* magazine.[43]

The trouncing by the critics and the bad word-of-mouth from the opening weekend crowds killed any chance the movie had of recouping its investment. Produced for an estimated $85 million, *Catwoman* made a disappointing $71 million at the worldwide box office. Halle tried to take it all in stride, but she was clearly hurt by all of the negative reviews and devastated by the hit she expected that her career would take as a result of all of the negative publicity. Hollywood can be an unforgiving place, and one bad movie could easily sink an actor's efforts to make another film. With opportunities for African-American actresses few and far between, Halle was rightfully concerned that the doors her Oscar-winning performance in *Monster's Ball* had opened may once again be closed—and this time, she may not get many more chances to prove that she was a bankable movie star and not a "gamble."

GETTING "RAZZED"

The critics who predicted that *Catwoman* would buy Halle a one-way ticket to the Razzies proved to be absolutely correct. Founded by John Wilson, the Golden Raspberry ("Razzie") Award Foundation was created to honor the worst of the worst in entertainment. Halle was named Worst Actress of the Year; she gamely showed up at the ceremony, held in Hollywood's Ivar Theatre in February 2005, to claim her award in person (she was the first actor to make such an appearance since comedian Tom Green won Worst Actor in 2001 for *Freddy Got Fingered*).

The *Catwoman* fallout may still have left a stinging sensation, but Halle proved she had not lost her sense of humor by making an appearance and mocking her Oscar speech in her acceptance. Wilson was kind to Berry, saying, "Don't get us wrong. She's a very talented actress, a very beautiful woman, who just made a mistake . . . we're only saying, we're so sorry you chose to do this."[44] Halle proved she was a good sport and showcased her ability to laugh at her failings.

Catwoman also won Razzies for Worst Director (Pitof), Worst Picture, and Worst Screenplay. Later, Halle admitted that winning the Razzie put her back in the position of being an underdog in Hollywood again—a position that she embraced, as it forced her to work harder.

NOTES

1. "Halle Berry Talks about Portraying Dorothy Dandridge," *JET*, July 26, 1999.

2. "Actress Could Face Hit-and-Run Charges," Associated Press State & Local Wire, March 1, 2000.

3. "Halle Berry Charged with Leaving the Scene of an Accident," Associated Press State & Local Wire, March 31, 2000.

4. Leslie Marshall, "Halle's Journey," *InStyle*, July 2000.

5. "Halle Berry Gets Probation, Fine for No-Contest Plea to Leaving Scene of Accident," Associated Press State & Local Wire, May 11, 2000.

6. Nancy Mills, "How Halle Got Her Groove Back," *Mail on Sunday* (London), April 1, 2007.

7. "X-Men: Who Will Save the World?" *Mirror* (London), August 11, 2000.

8. Andrew O'Hehir, "X-Men," *Salon.com*, July 14, 2000.

9. Gary Susman, "Stormy Marriage," *EW.com*, April 27, 2004.

10. "Portrait of a Lady," *USA Today*, January 20, 2001.

11. Christopher John Farley, "Halle Berry," *Time* magazine, January 13, 2002.

12. Jack Garner, "Halle Berry's Talent, Success Affords Her Carte Blanche in Getting Hard-to-Get Roles," Gannett News Service, February 6, 2002.

13. Peter Travers, "Review: Things We Lost in the Fire," *Rolling Stone*, RS 887, January 17, 2002.

14. "The Monsters That Haunt Halle," *Mirror* (London), June 7, 2002.

15. "Acting Coach Put Berry on Path to Oscar Win," *Detroit Free Press*, March 27, 2002.

16. "Halle's Second Act," *Variety*, August 15, 2005–August 21, 2005.

17. Samuel L. Jackson, "After Ten Years, a New Kind of Breakthrough," *Interview* magazine, March 2002.

18. Allison Samuels, "Angela's Fire," *Newsweek*, July 1, 2002.

19. Uju Asika, "Black America and the Oscars: A One-Night Stand?" *Salon.com*, March 29, 2002.

20. Ibid.

21. "Halle Berry Backlash Could Be Dangerous," *National Post*, July 5, 2002.

22. Stephen Farber, "Monster's Ball Review," Movieline, http://movieline.standard8media.com/reviews/monstersball.shtml.

23. Margaret A. McGurk, "Berry Astonishing in Ardent Monster's Ball," *Cincinnati Enquirer*, February 15, 2002.

24. Andrew Manning, "*Swordfish* review," Radio Free Movie Review, 2001.

25. "Beauty Jinx Laid to Rest with Oscar Win," *Associated Press*, November 19, 2002.

26. 74th Annual Academy Awards broadcast, original airdate March 24, 2002.

27. Jane Ridley and Claire Donnelly, "I Have No Love for My Dying Dad," *Mirror* (London), March 27, 2002.

28. Michael Atkinson, "A View to a Kill," *New York Village Voice*, November 19, 2002.

29. John Griffin, "Just Another Bond Flick," *Montreal Gazette*, November 22, 2002.

30. Paul Sims, "Halle: I Was on Brink of Suicide over Marriage Break-Up," *Evening Standard* (London), May 26, 2004.

31. Mark Reynolds, "Clean Slate for Halle's Cheating Husband," *Daily Telegraph* (Sydney, Australia), December 7, 2002.

32. Paul Kermode, "High-Octane Action by the Mutants," *Sunday Mail* (Brisbane, Australia), May 4, 2003.

33. "Halle Berry Splits from Eric Benet," *Toronto Globe and Mail*, October 3, 2003.

34. Reuters, "Halle's Husband Wants Money," *Toronto Sun*, June 5, 2004.

35. "Benet Says Fame Didn't Hurt His Marriage," Associated Press Online, July 15, 2004.

36. Ibid.

37. National Public Radio, "News & Notes: Eric Benet's New CD 'Hurricane,'" June 21, 2005.

38. http://www.imdb.com/name/nm0000932/bio.

39. Roger Ebert, *Gothika* film review, *rogertebert.com*, November 21, 2003.

40. Sharon Waxman, "Halle Berry Mixes Sexiness with Strength," *New York Times*, July 21, 2004.

41. Sarah Chauncey, *Catwoman* film review, *Reel.com*, www.reel.com/movie.asp?MID=139025&buy=closed&Tab=reviews&CID=13#tabs.

42. Gregory Weinkauf, "Meow Mixed," *Dallas Observer*, July 22, 2004.

43. Peter Dubradge, "Catwoman Review," *Premiere* magazine, http://www.metacritic.com/.

44. Beverley Lyons and Cath Bennett, "Razzie Berrry Delight," *Daily Record* (Glasgow, Scotland), February 28, 2005.

Chapter 6

THE ROAD TO FULFILLMENT

HALLE MAKES THE "BLUES"

Halle took a seat behind the scenes in 2005 to serve as an executive producer on the HBO original television movie *Lackawanna Blues*, which was based on Ruben Santiago-Hudson's autobiographical one-man dramatic play. The plot centers around a boarding house in the city of Lackawanna, New York, a fictional suburb of Buffalo. It is a coming-of-age tale that follows the story of a young boy left in the care of "Nanny" Crosby (played by S. Epatha Merkerson), the woman who runs the boarding house filled with colorful characters during the 1950s and 1960s in the time before Black integration. Santiago-Hudson adapted the screenplay and also played a small role in the film, which also starred Jeffrey Wright, Jimmy Smits, Terrence Howard, Rosie Perez, Marcus Carl Franklin, and Macy Gray.

Halle's coexecutive producer on *Lackawanna Blues* was her manager, Vincent Cirrincione, and she chose to produce the project because she and Santiago-Hudson were friends and she was a fan of his play. The movie premiered on HBO on February 12, 2005, and was both a critical success and a success in the ratings. "It's a joyful noise, a life-affirming celebration of the resilience of the human spirit," wrote *USA Today* critic Robert Bianco.[1] It went on to receive several nominations and awards, including a Directors Guild of America Award for George C. Wolfe, the celebrated Broadway stage director (*Jelly's Last Jam*, 1992, and *Angels in America*, 2003) who made his film directorial debut with *Lackawanna Blues*, a Primetime Emmy Award for Outstanding Lead Actress and a Golden Globe Award for Best Performance by an Actress in a Mini-Series or Motion Picture Made for Television for S. Epatha Merkerson, and an Outstanding Actor in a Motion Picture Image Award for Terrence Howard (a year before he was nominated for his star turn in the film *Hustle & Flow*, 2005).

"The film has moments of sadness and heartache...but 'Lackawanna' is at its best when it captures the fleeting joy of lost days," wrote *New York Times* critic Alessandra Stanley.[2]

QUEEN, REDUX?

In early 2005, it was reported that Halle would take on the role of a lifetime: that of Nefertiti, the legendary Egyptian queen who ruled alongside her husband, Pharaoh Akhenaten, from 1352 BC to 1336 BC and briefly ruled the ancient kingdom on her own after Akhenaten's death.

The project would give Halle the chance to play the type of epic role that actresses dream about. Indeed, not since Elizabeth Taylor portrayed Cleopatra in 1963 had an actress been offered a leading role in such a historic project.

History has looked kindly on *Cleopatra*, but when the movie was released, it was a big-budget box-office flop. Taylor's performance was universally panned, and the film was criticized for focusing too much on the visual elements and not enough on the story. Halle was determined to avoid some of the same mistakes and spent a significant portion of the next two years working on a script with Marc Forster, the director of *Monster's Ball* (2002).

"There's battle scenes and love," Halle excitedly told MTV news during an interview. "[It's about] a woman coming into her own ... about that time when Nefertiti was ruling her nation."[3]

It seemed fitting that Halle would play Nefertiti, whose name means "the beautiful woman has come,"[4] and that she would be reunited with Forster, who was to take the helm of this ambitious historical tale. However, the project never got off the ground, and the movie was never made.[5]

HALLE GETS ANIMATED

That same year, Halle would take a role in a big budget science fiction movie—but she would not have a single second of camera time. The film, *Robots* (2005), was an animated feature from the creators of *Ice Age*, the blockbuster cartoon released in 2002.

Halle voiced the role of Cappy, an attractive executive robot who becomes the love interest of Rodney Copperbottom (played by "*Star Wars Episode I*, 1999, and *Trainspotting*, 1996, star Ewan McGregor), an inventor in a world inhabited entirely by other robots and who challenges an evil corporate villain. Veteran actors Mel Brooks and Jim Broadbent also lent their vocal talents to the film's characters alongside McGregor, television actor Drew Carey ("*The Drew Carey Show*"), and teen actress Amanda Bynes.

Heralded for its breathtaking achievements in animation and shown in regular and IMAX theaters, *Robots* was a hit. ("A 100-percent guaranteed kid-pleaser that will also bowl over adults," said critic Tom Long in the *Detroit News*.[6] "Packed with unexpected charms," wrote Amy Biancolli in the *Houston Chronicle*.[7] Made for an estimated $75 million, *Robots* grossed $36 million during its opening weekend in the United States and went on to earn over $246 million worldwide.

WORKING WITH A QUEEN ON A CLASSIC

Halle had been a longtime fan of the novel *Their Eyes Were Watching God*, a classic piece of African-American literature written by author Zora Neale Hurston in 1937. Controversial when it was originally released, the story centers around Janie Crawford, a young African-American woman living in the small Black town of Eatonville, Florida, during the 1920s. Janie marries three different men (Mr. Killicks, Mayor Starks, and Tea Cake) and has been tried in court for the murder of one of them. The novel deftly explores the complicated issues of race, relationships, and feminism.

Oprah Winfrey, the billionaire talk-show host, actress, and producer, had long wanted to turn the book into a movie. Suzan-Lori Parks, the playwright who won the Pulitzer Prize for Drama in 2002 for her play "*Topdog/Underdog*" (starring Jeffrey Wright and Mos Def), was hired to write the screenplay. A friend of Halle's, Oprah called on the actress the day after she won the Academy Award and asked her to take the role of Janie. Oprah worried that Halle would turn her down, but Halle leapt at the opportunity. No need to audition or fly herself out for the chance to read for the role this time: the role was Halle's.

Their Eyes Were Watching God did well, airing on ABC in March 2005, and became the most-watched television movie to air on a network in more than five years. Nearly 27 million viewers tuned in to watch the broadcast.

A SHORT-LIVED ROMANCE

On the set of *Their Eyes Were Watching God*, Halle became close to one of her costars: Michael Ealy, a blue-eyed African-American actor who was born on August 3, 1973. Ealy (whose screen credits include roles in *Kissing Jessica Stein*, 2001, *Bad Company*, 2002, and *Miracle at St. Anna*, 2008), played the role of Tea Cake, a mysterious drifter that Halle's character runs away with.

Halle and Ealy (who was named to *People* magazine's "Sexiest Men Alive" list in 2002) created intense sexual chemistry on-screen, making their lover characters utterly believable and engaging to watch. As it turned out, there may have been more to those scenes than acting. And while life did not exactly imitate art—Halle did not run off with Ealy—the two did start dating while the movie was still filming. At the time, Ealy was seven years younger than Halle. While it was not quite a May-December romance, many speculated that it was a rebound relationship for Halle, a casual and fun fling for a woman who was still trying to get over the disappointment and heartbreak of her second failed marriage. Publicly, Ealy spoke very highly of Halle and credited her with teaching him how to handle fame. However, their romantic relationship was short-lived, and the two called it quits in 2005. Halle spoke very little about why their romance fizzled.

TAKING A STAND AGAINST THE PAPARAZZI

Halle and fellow actors Cameron Diaz, Lindsay Lohan, and Reese Witherspoon teamed up to join forces with the Los Angeles Police Department to take a formal stand against members of the paparazzi who practiced aggressive tactics in their pursuit of celebrity photos. While Halle and her peers acknowledged that regular attention from the media is part of their jobs, they sought out the cooperation of the authorities in taking further measures to prevent photographers from ambushing them and putting themselves and others at risk of physical harm.

An official investigation was launched to stop photographers from engaging in stealthy tactics, such as stealing schedules, hacking into computer files, impersonating police or security personnel, blocking license plate numbers, and forcing celebrities off the road in their vehicles.

A MODEL MEETING AND A DATE WITH DESTINY

In 2005, Halle became a spokesperson for Versace, the sexy high-fashion clothing label made famous by deceased designer Gianni Versace and taken over by his sister, Donatella. At a photo shoot in Los Angeles for the advertising campaign, Halle posed for sexy pictures with two male models, one of whom was a devastatingly handsome French Canadian named Gabriel Aubry.

Aubry, who was born in Montreal on January 4, 1976, had survived the turmoil of a rough childhood (he lived with five foster families from the age of 3 to 18) and was working as a cook at a ski resort in Quebec when he was discovered by a modeling and talent scout.[8] Aubry quickly entered the rarified ranks of male supermodels thanks to his slightly androgynous looks, piercing blue eyes, and lean, muscular physique. The six-foot-two model's previous work included high-profile campaigns and runway shows for Tommy Hilfiger, Hugo Boss, Ralph Lauren, and other top designers.

"I was at the [photo] shoot when they met," said Donatella Versace. "I know him very well. I pushed a little bit. I said, 'Why don't you go out together.' I said it in front of them. It went well at the shoot."[9] In an appearance on *The Oprah Winfrey Show*, Halle recounted how she was so attracted to Gabriel that she found it nearly impossible to concentrate on completing the photo shoot. "There were, like, just pheromones flying off the walls," she said.[10] One of the most memorable shots from the Versace campaign featured Halle leaning into Aubry in a moment that appears to capture an intimate dance. Halle's eyes are on the camera, and Aubry appears focused on her arm, but one can almost sense the physical attraction flying off the glossy page.

Up until that point, Halle had been convinced that she would not meet another man that she would want to be with until she was in her 50s, and she was sure that if she wanted to have a child, she would be doing it on her own as a single mother. But, physical attraction and age differences aside (Gabriel is 10 years Halle's junior), Halle was drawn to Gabriel's honesty, self-confidence, and integrity, and the two formed a fast friendship that quickly evolved into a full-fledged romance. The twosome first appeared together as a couple at the reopening of the Versace boutique in New York City on February 7, 2006. At the event, Halle looked very much like a woman in love— her face was aglow, and she and Gabriel were practically inseparable. By May, Halle was gushing about her newfound love. She confessed that Aubry had restored her faith in men and had her thinking about a future that had nothing to do with being on a movie set:

> It's so new and fresh . . . but I've reached a point in my life where I have realized that I need more than a career . . . I think the next chapter in my life is family and children. I mean, I'm going to be 40 in August, for God's sake. I've done many things in my career that have made me feel fulfilled, but this personal challenge is of much more substance.[11]

Together with business partner Stephane Bibeau, Aubry opened Café Fuego in New York City's East Village neighborhood on St. Mark's Place in October 2006. The Cuban restaurant boasted a Spanish Colonial-inspired interior featuring a romantic fireplace and artful furnishings reportedly bought via eBay. Halle was there on opening night to support her boyfriend's endeavor, which served up traditional Cuban dishes including *ropa vieja* alongside fusion fare (a Cobb salad with black beans, for instance). However, New York City is a tough place to run a restaurant. Hundreds open every year, and the competition, combined with high rents and skyrocketing expenses, can sink even the best eateries. Café Fuego had a strong opening and a great location, but the buzz quickly wore off and it would close two years later.[12]

HALLE BERRY, POP SINGER?

In December 2006, the rumor mill kicked into high gear about Halle. This time, it had nothing to do with a movie, or a man, or an accident . . . it was about her supposed singing ambitions. *Rolling Stone* magazine reported that the actress was set to release an album titled *Halle* in early 2007.[13] Superproducers Timbaland (best known for his work crafting hit songs for Justin Timberlake and Nelly Furtado) and Scott Storch (who has provided beats for Chris Brown, Beyoncé, and 50 Cent) had reportedly worked with Halle on her solo debut.

Were the rumors true? Halle had never expressed a desire to sing before—was it possible that the small amount of singing she had done playing vocalists in *Why Do Fools Fall in Love?* (1998) and *Introducing Dorothy Dandridge* (1999) had sparked a new ambition? No one knows, but one thing is for sure: an album was never released, and Halle has never commented about it publicly. And while Halle would not have been the first actress-turned-singer—Minnie Driver, Scarlett Johanssen, and Julie Delpy have all released albums—most have been unsuccessful, and the possibility that the Oscar-winner would choose to moonlight as a wannabe pop star was widely considered a bad move.

CLOSING THE X-MEN CHAPTER

The *X-Men* movie franchise had become a pop culture juggernaut that would not be denied, and a third and final installment in the series was directed by Brett Ratner (*Rush Hour*, 1998, and *Money Talks*, 1997) and was released in theaters on May 26, 2006.

Titled *X-Men: The Last Stand*, the movie focused on the character of Jean Grey (Famke Jannsen) who is killed but is reborn as the Phoenix. The Phoenix is bestowed with new powers that she cannot fully control, and she joins forces with Magneto and kills Professor X. The remaining X-Men—including Halle's character, Storm—band together to destroy Magneto and Phoenix and to fight the pull of a "cure" that will make them human—but will also take away their superpowers.

The Last Stand was panned by many major critics as the weakest film in the *X-Men* franchise, but the movie-going public paid little attention: the third *X-Men* was the most successful film of the three, earning a mind-boggling $234 million in the United States and $455 million worldwide. Based on that success, it certainly seemed as though the franchise could go on forever, but all of the loose ends in the storyline had been tied up and everyone involved was ready to move on to other projects.

Capping off the success of X-Men for Halle was a series of incidents that occurred while she was traveling to promote the film. First, she broke her toe while running to catch a flight after attending the Cannes Film Festival in France to New York City. Not willing to sacrifice her style, she was seen wearing heels in the days that followed. Next, while Halle was in New York, she took an ill-fated promotional trip aboard the U.S. Navy ship USS *Kearsarge* during Fleet Week. Halle ate a meal that included shrimp before she participated in a meet-and-greet with many of the sailors stationed on the ship. During the proceedings, one sailor offered up a proposal of marriage, flattering Halle, but shortly after that she suddenly felt ill and broke out in an itchy rash. She was immediately taken down below to the hospital infirmary, where the ship's doctor gave her some Benadryl. Halle took a nap and quickly recovered.

A TRUE HOLLYWOOD STAR

The year 2006 also marked the year that Halle would join yet another exclusive club: The Hollywood Reporter's annual Star Salary Top 10 List. Halle came in at number six on the list, thanks to the $14 million she made in salaries from her movies that year.

Ahead of her on the list were Nicole Kidman ($16 to $17 million per film), Reese Witherspoon ($15 million), Renée Zellweger ($15 million), Drew Barrymore ($15 million), and Cameron Diaz ($15 million). Below Halle on the list were Charlize Theron ($10 million), Angelina Jolie ($10 million), Kirsten Dunst ($8 to $10 million), and Jennifer Aniston ($8 million).

April 4, 2007, was a beautiful day in Los Angeles. The sun was shining, a light breeze filled the air, and Halle Berry stood outside the Kodak Theater surrounded by hundreds of adoring fans. She looked lovely, her long, straight hair flowing down her back and a formfitting black dress accentuated with black lace hugging her curves.

The occasion was four years overdue: Halle was at the Kodak Theater to receive a star on the Hollywood Walk of Fame, an honor given to actors and other film industry professionals in recognition of their career achievements. Halle's star—number 2,333 among the concrete markers set into the sidewalks on and around Hollywood Boulevard—had originally been awarded to Halle four years beforehand, but the actress was reportedly too busy with back-to-back film projects and promotional tours to attend the formal ceremony.

Halle's proud mother was in attendance for the proceedings, as was Halle's boyfriend Gabriel Aubry, who stood discreetly to the side to make sure the attention was on Halle's star and not their relationship. Samuel L. Jackson, Halle's first costar, was also present. In her remarks, Halle promised not to give another teary-eyed acceptance speech (referring to her memorably weepy Academy Award–winning moment) before she thanked all of the people in her life that had gotten her to that point—including Jackson, whom she referred to as her first acting teacher. "He helped me to believe in me," Halle said of Jackson at the ceremony. "I didn't know what I was doing, and I'll never forget how he took me under his wing." Halle later called her mother up to the podium (who had joked earlier that people would be walking all over her daughter's name) and recalled the moment shortly after her arrival in Los Angeles 15 years ago when she walked down Hollywood Boulevard and was inspired by the names she saw pressed into the concrete. She remembered how she had stood on the star of Dorothy Dandridge. "I felt the pain, I felt the struggle, I felt the joy, I felt the struggle, and I felt the pride that she had a star on the Walk of Fame . . . it's my honor to be a part of such an illustrious group."

Halle later bent down to kiss her star as it was placed in the ground and lay down on the red carpet next to it to pose for photos. Her star was yet another high point in her now-fabled career.

In just over a week after Halle received her star on the Hollywood Walk of Fame, her dramatic suspense movie *Perfect Stranger* (2007) opened in theaters. Halle had the lead role of Rowena Price, a journalist who goes undercover as a temporary employee to prove that Harrison Hill, a wealthy advertising agency owner (played by *Die Hard* (1988) and *Moonlighting* (1985) star Bruce Willis), is the killer of her best friend, Grace (Nicki Lynn Aycox), who met Hill in an Internet chat room and had a steamy affair with him. Rowena then proceeds to flirt with Hill in an attempt to get closer to him and find evidence of the murder on his computer.

The high-tech thriller, which was filmed on location in New York City, also starred actors Giovanni Ribisi (*Boiler Room*, 2000) as Rowena's friend and colleague and Gary Dourdan (*CSI*) as Rowena's lover. The plot was filled with twists and turns, but failed to catch the attention of the moviegoing public. *Perfect Stranger* made a disappointing $23 million at the box office in the United States and went on to earn over $53 million in the worldwide market. "A routine thriller," quipped *Los Angeles Times* movie critic Kenneth Turan.[14] "For those who are interested in Berry as both an actress and screen presence, this is one of the most satisfying films she has ever made. It capitalizes on her strengths and she owns the picture, from start to finish," wrote *San Francisco Chronicle* movie reviewer Mick LaSalle.[15]

ON THE MOMMY TRACK

Despite all of the success Halle had enjoyed in her career, there was one thing that she felt was missing—a baby. In 2006, Halle told an interviewer on the television newsmagazine *Extra* that she would adopt a child one day even if she had to do it without a romantic partner by her side.

Halle revealed on Oprah that she and Gabriel had been inspired by her role as a mother in her upcoming film *Things We Lost in the Fire* (2007) and had been trying for months to conceive a child together the old-fashioned way.[16] It was during the preproduction of the John Singleton–directed movie *Tulia* (2009)—in which Halle would portray an attorney defending a group of Black men wrongfully accused of dealing drugs and be reunited on the screen with her *Monster's Ball* costar Billy Bob Thornton) that Halle found out that she was pregnant. Production on the film was shut down. In September 2007, Halle sent a text message to her close friend and *Access Hollywood* anchor Nancy O'Dell, who would break the news on her entertainment news program[17] that she was expecting Gabriel's baby and was three months pregnant at the time.

Days later, Halle was involved in a car accident. She was allegedly being chased by an aggressive car filled with paparazzi eager to take her picture when she smashed up her car, causing $8,000 worth of damage to her vehicle. No other cars were involved in the incident, and no one was hurt. Halle was violently jolted in the accident and was concerned about her baby, but both mother-to-be and unborn child were unharmed. Halle was reportedly incensed that the paparazzi drove off (in cars without license plates, so they could not be reported to the police) and the news media failed to report the story.[18]

"So there I was stuck with my crashed-up car wondering if this somehow impacted my pregnancy and feeling totally helpless and violated and I had no recourse against anyone," Halle said later.[19]

A month later, Halle's latest film, *Things We Lost in the Fire*, opened in theaters. The dramatic film paired the actress with Benicio del Toro, who won the Academy Award for Best Supporting Actor for his role in *Traffic* in 2001. The movie was the first English-language film directed by Danish writer/director Susanne Bier. Halle plays Audrey Burke, the married mother of two young children who is forced to come to terms with the tragic, unexpected death of her loving husband (played by David Duchovny). Drowning in sorrow, Audrey turns to the one person who knew her husband longer than she did—his heroin-addicted best friend, Jerry (del Toro). Audrey asks Jerry to come and live with her, and the two forge a complicated relationship as they try to rebuild their lives and cope with his drug demons and her broken heart.

The role of Audrey was yet another role Halle would play that was not written with an African-American actress in mind. "I hoped maybe they would be able to see outside the box," Halle said of the filmmakers. "My biggest fear got put to rest when I realized the director, Susanne Bier, did not care one ounce about the color of my skin."[20]

In an ironic case of life imitating art, the London premiere of *Things We Lost in the Fire* was delayed after a fire in the kitchen of a nearby restaurant in Leicester Square, the site of the location where the film was scheduled to be screened, went up in flames. The block was shut down until firefighters were able to get the blaze under control. At the same time, wildfires raged through Southern California, wiping out hundreds of homes and causing thousands of people to evacuate. Halle worried about the home she had in the area as well as the safety of her neighbors.

It was hoped that Halle's performance in *Things We Lost in the Fire* would bring back the kind of critical acclaim that she received for *Monster's Ball* (2001), but the reviews were decidedly mixed. A review in *USA Today* read, "The movie makes some missteps, most of them in pacing and length, and the story veers occasionally into melodrama, but it is saved by the powerful performance of Benicio Del Toro."[21] It probably did not help that the film was released on the same weekend as eight other new films (including the Ben Affleck–directed drama *Gone Baby Gone* (2007) and *Rendition* (2007), a terrorist thriller starring

Meryl Streep, Reese Witherspoon, and Jake Gyllenhaal) and may have been overlooked amid all of the competition for moviegoers' attention. Halle did win several minor awards for her performance, including Best Actress at the Palm Springs Film Festival, but was snubbed by the Oscars.

Halle returned from the London premier eager to settle into impending motherhood. Like many pregnant women undergoing hormonal changes, Halle experienced food cravings—mostly bread and salt—but the expectant mother stayed healthy by eating a balanced diet and working out with light weights, swimming, exercising on an elliptical trainer, and taking prenatal yoga classes. Gabriel, meanwhile, read baby manuals and parenting books to prepare for fatherhood. The two threw themselves into preparing their homes in Malibu and in Hollywood Hills for their impending bundle of joy, and they hired designers from the boutique NoMi to decorate both nurseries.

Halle remained very stylish throughout her pregnancy, taking advantage of the voluminous, high-waisted fashions filling stores that year to showcase her expanding belly. In fact, she and Aubry were named "Best-Dressed Couple" by *People* magazine that year.

A PUBLIC MISSTEP

When Halle was four months pregnant, she appeared on *The Tonight Show with Jay Leno*. Halle had brought some photos of herself to show Leno that had been digitally manipulated on Photo Booth, a computer program that alters photos and makes them appear distorted, for fun. One of the photos showed Halle with a large, distorted nose, and Halle made the comment on the air that the photo was of "her Jewish cousin." Her attempt at a joke got a lukewarm laugh at the taping of the show and prompted Leno to comment, "I'm glad you said that and not me."[22]

Hours later, Halle regretted her comment and called Leno to ask him to remove the joke from the show's broadcast. He "bleeped" out the word "Jewish" and the show aired as scheduled, but the damage had been done.

Members of the Jewish community were incensed by Halle's comment, and Halle was appropriately embarrassed. She explained that she was joking around before the show with three of her staff members who happened to be Jewish, and one of them made the "Jewish cousin" joke. The comment seemed harmless and was fresh in her mind when she went on the air, so she repeated the joke without thinking of the ramifications.[23] Halle issued a public apology for her insensitive statement, and the incident quickly blew over.

A POLITICAL DECLARATION

It was not all about the baby during her nine months of pregnancy: Halle announced her public support of presidential candidate Barack Obama, the African-American senator from Illinois who was running as a member of the Democratic Party. Halle donated $2,300 (the maximum amount allowed for the Democratic primary) to his campaign (as did fellow actors including George Clooney, Jennifer Aniston, and Jaime Foxx) and continued to show her support at fund-raisers and other events designed to encourage people to vote for Obama. The paparazzi also caught Halle out on several occasions wearing T-shirts that proclaimed her support for the candidate. When Obama won the election, Halle was one of several high-profile celebrities who attended the inaugural festivities in Washington, D.C., and was one of a handful of Hollywood power players (including actor Tom Hanks and director Steven Spielberg) who donated $50,000 each to his Inaugural Fund.[24]

INTRODUCING NAHLA ARIELA AUBRY

Like most women, Halle was terrified about the act of giving birth, but she also had something else to worry about: her diabetes. According to the American Diabetes Association, women who have been diagnosed with diabetes prior to pregnancy may have a higher risk of having a child with birth defects.[25] Halle did a good job of keeping her condition under control throughout her pregnancy, and on Saturday, March 16, 2008, she gave birth to a seven pound, four ounce baby girl.[26]

Halle was exhausted but ecstatic, and she and Gabriel left Los Angeles' Cedars-Sinai Medical Center days later with their new bundle of joy. Their daughter left the hospital without a name—Halle and Gabriel decided that they wanted to be surprised by the sex of their baby at birth, and they wanted to get to know who she was before they decided what to call her. Weeks later, baby Aubry's name was announced: Nahla Ariela. Pronounced "NAW-lah ARE-ee-EL-uh," her names reportedly mean "a drink of water" and "lion of God."[27]

LIFE AFTER BABY

Shortly after baby Nahla was born, it was rumored that Halle was in the running to play the role of Blanche DuBois in a London stage production of the classic 1947 Tennessee Williams play A *Streetcar Named Desire*. That project never happened, but Halle has expressed a desire to expand her craft by acting on the stage and hoped that she would find the right project in which to do so in the future.

Aubry, for his part, was not about to become a Hollywood house-husband who loafed around the mansion and spent his wife's money as if it was going out of style (like singer Britney Spears's ex-husband, Kevin Federline). He continued to model, and in 2008 he signed an exclusive contract to become the face of Calvin Klein's menswear. That same year, Aubry appeared in a high-profile commercial for Macy's Department Stores. He did not utter a single word as he made his way through the store in the television spot, but he is memorably ogled by both singer Mariah Carey and business mogul Martha Stewart while a jealous Donald Trump pouts.

Meanwhile, Halle prepared to add the role of fragrance mogul to her already impressive list of credits. Already a fan of mixing her own fragrances for her own personal use, Halle signed a deal with Coty Inc., a cosmetics company, to develop a range of perfumes and appear in advertising campaigns to promote the scents. Halle would join the esteemed company of other celebrities who have signed similar perfume deals, including Jennifer Lopez, Gwen Stefani, Sarah Jessica Parker, and David and Victoria Beckham. All of their respective fragrances have made millions, and hopes were high that Halle's would do similar business. The first of Halle's fragrances, to be called, simply, "Halle," would be a blend of mimosa, fig, and other scents and was expected to hit department stores such as J. C. Penney and move into mass market retail stores in 2009. Halle was directly involved in all aspects of the development of the fragrance, including visiting the lab to test and mix the scent from conception to final product.

Eager to get her body back into prepregnancy shape, Halle hired celebrity personal trainer Ramona Braganza (who also worked with actresses Anne Hathaway and Jessica Biel) and started on a tough regimen of 60-minute workouts five days a week that included three cardiovascular segments followed by a strength-training routine to help tighten her abdominals and tone her legs.[28] Her efforts paid off with a vengeance: just six weeks after giving birth, Halle was photographed at an auction in Los Angeles looking trim and sleek in an empire waist, leopard print minidress.

Bucking the trend of other Hollywood celebrities—such as Angelina Jolie and Brad Pitt, Nicole Richie, and Christina Aguilera—who chose to sell photos of their newborns to magazines, Halle went out of her way for months to keep Nahla out of the limelight. Desperate members of the paparazzi tried in vain to be first to get a photo of the elusive Halle and her baby, but to no avail. It was not until late July 2008 that Halle and baby were first snapped together—though Halle was upset because she alleged that the photographer came onto the backyard of her private property to get the shot. She hired a lawyer and filed a suit to get the pictures removed from the Internet and attempted to prosecute the photographer responsible for taking and distributing the photos.

By the fall, Halle and Nahla came out of hiding and were spotted at an outing at the Los Angeles Zoo with her mother, Judith, and Gabriel; later mother and daughter were snapped in a public park sharing a ride together on a swing. With parents as attractive as Halle and Gabriel, Nahla was sure to be a gorgeous baby—and indeed she was, with expressive blue eyes, a cherubic face, and wavy, thick hair.

WILL THEY OR WON'T THEY?

It was thought that Halle planned to marry Gabriel, and the rumor mill kicked into high gear when Halle was spotted at the Entertainment Industry Foundation's Revlon Run/Walk in May 2008 wearing an impressive-looking ring on her left hand. However, it turned out that the ring was not an engagement ring that had once belonged to Gabriel's grandmother—instead, it was a bauble that Halle bought for herself as a fashion statement.

Halle had previously said that she would never marry again, and that was not about to change because she and Aubry were happy and committed to one another. "It's just that now I've come to a place where I think two people can share their lives without the ring, with-out the piece of paper," she said.[29] Her attitude about marriage is a bit of a throwback, as more and more of her contemporaries—includ-ing Angela Bassett, Nicole Kidman, and Gwyneth Paltrow—decided that saying "I do" was as official a declaration of love as one could get. However, Halle's way of thinking is not exactly a new thing in Hollywood. For decades, such actresses as Goldie Hahn and Susan Sarandon, who had both experienced failed marriages, decided that when they had found the men they wanted to spend the rest of their lives with (actors Kurt Russell and Tim Robbins, respectively), a wed-ding and a marriage license would not do anything to strengthen their bond. Hahn and Sarandon's nontraditional unions have lasted longer than the formal marriages of most of their peers, proving that for Halle, it was possible to stay happy, committed, and in love and skip the wedding rings, the marriage license, and exchanging of vows.

Unlike the arrangement Madonna had with Carlos Leon (the father of her first child, Lola), Halle was determined to raise her child with Aubry present, marriage or not. And Aubry has indeed become an active parent and a stabilizing force in Halle's life. Aubry's family in Canada has embraced the newest members of their extended family, and true to his French Canadian roots, Aubry has already voiced his intentions that his daughter grow up learning to speak French as well as English.

JUST THE BEGINNING

Decades ago in Hollywood, when an actress had a child, it was understood that she would not be seen on the big screen again for awhile and, more often than not, parenthood usually marked the end of her career. That same thinking did not apply to Hollywood fathers, of course. As part of that long-held double standard, male actors could be seen happily posing with their sons and daughters in publicity photos while continuing to act, but most actresses were forced to keep their kids out of sight, lest they be seen as less than appealing, or worse, too old to play certain parts.

By the time Halle gave birth to Nahla, she was part of a new wave of Hollywood moms who made having children not only celebrated, but fashionable. Angelina Jolie was one of the first actresses who made motherhood sexy when she chose to take a break from work to adopt two children and have one of her own (with actor Brad Pitt) in 2005, and her "baby bump" got her more press than her acting roles ever did. Reece Witherspoon, Julia Roberts, Gwyneth Paltrow, and Madonna quickly followed suit.

Halle certainly was not planning to let motherhood end her career, but she did concede that becoming a mother might cool interest in her as a sex symbol (this turned out not to be the case). From her perspective, that would be a good thing—she could finally say goodbye to those ingénue and bombshell roles that were not known for their depth and character development, and ease into meatier, edgier parts that would challenge her as an actress and build on the respect she earned for her Oscar-winning role in *Monster's Ball*. "I think I'll actually find better roles," she said. However, Halle was not planning to become the kind of celebrity mom who leaves her child behind to be raised by a nanny while she is off on movie sets 11 months of the year. "I'm definitely going to work less. I used to put so much pressure on myself to succeed that it often made me very unhappy in my personal life. I felt on the verge of burning out three or four years ago."[30]

However, Halle could not have been more wrong about waning public interest in her sexy status. In November 2008—a mere six months after Nahla was born—Halle was named the sexiest woman alive by *Esquire* magazine. She graced the magazine's cover sitting in a chair while wearing a black suit jacket, powder blue tie, and a black bra, a seductive smirk on her face and her hair in long, tousled ringlets. The flirtatious pose was an homage to a similar one that former U.S. President Bill Clinton struck on the men's magazine December 2000 cover. In the article, Halle confessed that she liked her body better since she became a mother and believed that sexiness is a state of mind—about loving yourself in your most unlovable moments.[31]

ON THE HORIZON

Would there be life after baby for Halle? All signs were pointing to a resounding yes. In 2008, Halle joined the ranks of fellow celebrities Jennifer Lopez, Mariah Carey, and Britney Spears when she announced that she would be selling a fragrance. During the two years she took off between filming her last movie and having Nahla, Halle worked on the development of her signature scent, "Halle by Halle Berry." Halle called the creation of the perfume, which features notes of mimosa and fig, her "second baby."[32]

Halle was also honored at *Elle* magazine's 15th Annual Women in Hollywood Tribute, a star-studded event that also recognized Nicole Kidman, Jane Fonda, Sigourney Weaver, Salma Hayek, Anne Hathaway, and Isla Fisher for their contributions to the film industry.

Work on *Tulia*, which had been suspended when Halle found out she was pregnant, was scheduled to resume in 2008. The film is being produced by Halle's own production company, Bellah Films ("Halle B" spelled backward). Also in the works were projects that Halle held close to her heart. One was *Nappily Ever After*, a movie based on a popular 2000 book by Trisha R. Thomas. It tells the story of Venus Johnston, an advertising executive who tires of her high-maintenance hairstyle (Venus has her naturally kinky, or "nappy," hair chemically straightened) and her noncommittal boyfriend. She shaves off her hair, kicks her boyfriend to the curb, and struggles to start a new life as she deals with racism and sexual harassment at the office.

The scene in which Venus shaves her head will be recreated in the film, and Halle planned to shave her own hair for real to accurately depict the pivotal moment in the character's life. Halle has admitted that she is terrified of going bald, but that the prospect is also a little exciting as well.[33] *Nappily Ever After* was scheduled to arrive in theaters in 2010.

Another film in the works had Halle selected to portray a Black woman with multiple-personality disorder in the psychological drama *Frankie and Alice* (2009). One of her character's alter egos is a White racist.[34] In October 2008, she was headed to Vancouver to start filming the movie and had been seen carrying around a book titled *Diagnosis and Treatment of Multiple Personality Disorder*, presumably as research for the role. Halle was also working as an executive producer on the film and had brought along daughter Nahla so that they would not be separated while she was working on the film. Paparazzi also caught Halle on set looking decidedly unglamorous in a costume featuring an unflattering curly wig, torn fishnet pantyhose, and a skimpy leather outfit held together by metal rings. Her first movie since 2007's *Things We Lost in the Fire*, *Frankie and Alice* also stars Stellan Skarsgård

(*Angels & Demons*, 2009), Chandra Wilson (*Grey's Anatomy*), and Phylicia Rashād (*The Cosby Show*) and was tentatively scheduled for a 2009 release.

In *Class Act*, a movie that was in production in 2008, Halle had been tapped to play Tierney Cahill, a schoolteacher in Nevada who decides to run for Congress and get her class of sixth-grade students at Sarah Winnemucca Elementary School to help her with her campaign. The movie, based on Cahill's real-life story, follows Cahill as she teaches her class a lesson in civics and tells them that anyone living in America can run for a political office. Her students do not believe her, so, to prove them wrong, she runs for the District 2 Congressional seat in an attempt to unseat the popular incumbent senator. With little money and no political experience, Cahill got 34 percent of the vote— not enough to win, but enough to teach her sixth-graders an important lesson. *Class Act* was being produced by DreamWorks SKG, the powerful movie studio helmed by Steven Spielberg, Jeffery Katzenberg, and David Geffen, and was to be directed by Doug Atchison, who also wrote the screenplay.

The fact that Cahill is White will mark yet another historic moment in Halle's career: while she has portrayed many fictional characters that were originally written for White actresses, by playing Cahill, Halle will become the first African-American actress to appear as a real-life White woman in a biographical film. In real life, Cahill is married to an African-American man and has biracial children.

Also rumored for Halle is a leading role in the action film *Who Is Doris Payne?*. Halle would play the role of Payne, a talented thief with an international criminal career who spent over 50 years stealing valuable jewels. That movie was scheduled for release in 2010.

On the production side, Halle's company was also attached to an unnamed project starring the R&B singer Alicia Keys and *Mixed*, a series for the Lifetime cable television network. Halle was not slated to star in the television show, which was said to be based on Halle's own experiences growing up as the daughter of a biracial couple. And rumors resurfaced in Hollywood that Halle was once again trying to make a big-budget biopic of "Nefertiti." Her *Monster's Ball* director Marc Forster was believed to be back in the role of director, and Halle's production company was attempting to secure financing for the movie.

THE REAL HALLE BERRY

In August 2008, Halle celebrated her 42nd birthday in style: she attended a concert by blue-eyed soul singer Robin Thicke at the House of Blues in Los Angeles—a performance that ended with Thicke singing an a cappella version of "Happy Birthday" to a beaming and radiant Halle.

Halle definitely appeared to be in a happy place: according to Aubry, he and Halle were planning to add at least one more child to their growing family. "We are working on that," he told Usmagazine.com. "She is the best mom that anyone could ask for—or wish for."[35] Halle also reportedly bought a million-dollar house near Aubry's relatives in the small town of St. Hippolyte, Quebec, located on 63 acres of land and overlooking picturesque Molson Lake, in order to spend time near family. The property is the third home in Halle's real-estate portfolio—she already owned a four-bedroom estate in Hollywood Hills that she bought for $6 million from Frankie Muniz (star of the popular 1990s television sitcom *Malcolm in the Middle*) and an $8 million property in Malibu, California, that she uses as a personal retreat.

In an attempt to expand her personal horizons and spend more time with Aubry, Halle has taken up the game of golf—a pastime that Aubry loves. Reluctant at first to learn a sport that she deemed boring, Halle has learned to appreciate it and now enjoys "hitting the links" with her boyfriend every chance she gets.[36]

Halle continued her charitable work in earnest, participating in the annual Revlon Run/Walk and on "Stand Up to Cancer," a celebrity fund-raising effort that solicited donations from the public in an event that aired on all of the major television networks simultaneously on September 5, 2008. Halle also continued to lend her support to Barack Obama's 2008 presidential campaign and appeared in "Don't Vote," a star-studded advertisement alongside Leonardo DiCaprio, Jamie Foxx, Jennifer Aniston, and other celebrities who used humor and reverse psychology to encourage young people to go to the polls in November.

Halle also kept up her support for domestic violence survivors by donating the one-of-a-kind, hand-carved rose gold cuff bracelet that she wore in the ad campaign for her fragrance line to the Jenesse Center, which put the bracelet up for auction on CharityBuzz.com. All of the proceeds from the bracelet's sale went to fund the domestic violence intervention program.

After years spent fighting for roles and recognition, it appeared that Halle Berry had finally hit a career stride. Now she is in control, calling the shots and green-lighting her own projects. She has become a power player, a mogul, an international brand. When you hear the name Halle, you know that there can be only one.

And the freedom that comes with success has allowed the actress to find out who she really is and become comfortable in her own skin. Halle has opened herself to a romantic relationship that is based upon mutual respect and understanding and put herself in a place where she finally felt comfortable enough to have the child she has always dreamed of having.

It is an enviable life, for sure: a beautiful and successful actress, in love with a handsome and down-to-earth model, mother to an adorable daughter. Surely Halle has enough money so that she would never have to work again, but because she loves what she does—the craft of acting—she can choose to do things that will challenge and expand her skills.

Is it really possible for a woman in Hollywood to have everything she wants? Probably not. But for Halle Berry, it is quite possible that, at long last, she has everything she needs.

NOTES

1. Robert Bianco, "HBO's Bright 'Lackawanna Blues' Holds Sway," *USA Today*, February 11, 2005.

2. Alessandra Stanley, "Holding Fast to Dreams in a Destitute World," *New York Times*, February 11, 2005.

3. "Halle Berry's 'Nefertiti' Will Have 'Epic Quality' to It," http://moviesblog.mtv.com/2007/10/15/halle-berrys-nefertiti-will-have-epic-quality-to-it/.

4. *Who Was Nefertiti: Nefertiti Discovered*, Discovery Channel documentary.

5. Gary Sussman, "Pyramid Scheme," *Entertainment Weekly*, February 16, 2005.

6. http://www.rottentomatoes.com/m/robots/?critic=creamcrop.

7. Amy Biancolli, "Robots: Go to Showtimes," *Houston Chronicle*, August 5, 2005, http://www.chron.com/disp/story.mpl/ae/movies/reviews/3079076.html.

8. Doug Camilli, "Montrealer Hasn't Been Home Much: Spending His Time in Love with Halle Berry," *Montreal Gazette*, March 15, 2006.

9. Jeffrey Slonim, "Dontalla Versace: Halle Berry's Baby 'Fantastic Looking,'" People.com, March 19, 2008.

10. "Halle's Having a Baby," *The Oprah Winfrey Show*, original airdate October 2, 2007.

11. John Hiscock, "Halle Storms Back," *Mirror* (London), May 26, 2006.

12. "Café Fuego," nymag.com/listings/restaurant/cafe-fuego/.

13. "Halle Berry Set to Ruin Reputation, Puffy Wants Dancing & Singing Boys and More," December 11, 2006, http://www.rollingstone.com/rockdaily/index.php/2006/12/11/halle-berry-set-to-ruin-reputation-puffy-wants-dancing-singing-boys-and-more/.

14. Kenneth Turan, *Perfect Stranger* movie review, *Los Angeles Times*, April 13, 2007.

15. Mick LaSalle, "Halle's Back, In Hot Pursuit," *San Francisco Chronicle*, April 13, 2007.

16. oprah.com.

17. Access Hollywood.com.

18. Tavis Smiley transcript *Halle Berry*, original airdate October 19, 2007, http://www.pbs.org/kcet/tavissmiley/archive/200710/20071019_berry.html.

19. Ibid.

20. "I Think I Have a Way With Children," *Daily Post* (Liverpool), January 25, 2008.

21. Studio Briefing, October 19, 2007.

22. Fox News, "Halle Berry Sorry for Joke about Jewish Noses," http://www.foxnews.com/story/0,2933,304299,00.html.

23. Ibid.

24. "Inaugural Donors Gave Obama $53 Mil," Bloomberg News, April 22, 2009.

25. "Gestational Diabetes," American Diabetes Association Web site.

26. "Halle's Daughter," *AccessHollywood.com*, March 20, 2008.

27. "Halle Berry Reveals Daughter's Name," *Usmagazine.com*, March 18, 2008.

28. Jenny Sundel and Stephen M. Silverman, "Halle Berry's Body after Baby Workout Revealed," *People.com*, May 13, 2008.

29. "Pregnant, But No Wedding," *Gazette* (Montreal), September 6, 2007.

30. World Entertainment News Network, May 29, 2008.

31. "An Acceptance Speech by Halle Berry," *Esquire*, November 2008, p. 112.

32. "Halle Berry Launches Perfume," *Metro* (London), October 4, 2008.

33. "Halle Berry to Shave Her Head in Movie," WENN, April 5, 2007.

34. Dave McNary, "Halle Berry Set for Frankie & Alice," *Daily Variety*, April 18, 2008.

35. "Halle Berry's Beau: 'We Are Working on Having More Children,'" *Usmagazine.com*, October 7, 2008.

36. "Anything for Love," *Canada National Post*, April 14, 2009.

Appendix A

HALLE BERRY FILMOGRAPHY AND TELEVISION APPEARANCES

Things We Lost in the Fire (2007) Audrey Burke

Perfect Stranger (2007) Rowena Price

X-Men: The Last Stand (2006) Storm/Ororo Munroe

Robots (2005) Cappy (voice)

Oprah Winfrey Presents ... Their Eyes Were Watching God (2005)
(made-for-television movie) Janie Starks

Catwoman: The Game (2004) Patience Phillips/Catwoman (voice)

Catwoman (2004) Patience Phillips/Catwoman

Gothika (2003) Miranda Grey

X2: X-Men United (2003) Storm/Ororo Munroe

Die Another Day (2002) Jinx

Monster's Ball (2001) Leticia Musgrove

Swordfish (2001) Ginger Knowles

X-Men (2000) Storm/Ororo Munroe

Introducing Dorothy Dandridge (1999) (made-for-television movie)
Dorothy Dandridge

Why Do Fools Fall in Love (1998) Zola Taylor

Bulworth (1998) Nina

Frasier (television series, 1 episode, 1998) episode: "Room Service"
(1998) Betsy (voice)

Oprah Winfrey Presents: The Wedding (1998) (made-for-television
movie) Shelby Coles

Mad TV Host (1 episode, 1998)

B.A.P.S (1997) Nisi
The Rich Man's Wife (1996) Josie Potenza
Race the Sun (1996) Miss Sandra Beecher
Executive Decision (1996) Jean
Losing Isaiah (1995) Khaila Richards
Solomon & Sheba (1995) (made-for-television movie) Nikhaule/Queen
    Sheba
The Flintstones (1994) Miss Sharon Stone
The Program (1993) Autumn Haley
Father Hood (1993) Kathleen Mercer
Queen (1993) (television miniseries) Queen
Boomerang (1992) Angela Lewis
Knots Landing (television series) Debbie Porter (21 episodes, 1991–
    1992)
The Last Boy Scout (1991) Cory
Strictly Business (1991) Natalie
Jungle Fever (1991) Vivian
They Came from Outer Space (television series) (1 episode, 1991
    episode: "Hair Today, Gone Tomorrow," Rene
A Different World (television series) (1 episode, 1991) episode: "Love,
    Hillman-Style," Jacklyn
Amen (television series) (1 episode, 1991) episode: "Unforgettable,"
    Claire
Living Dolls (television series) Emily Franklin (12 episodes, 1989)

Halle Berry Producer Credits
2009 *Frankie and Alice* (Producer)
2005 *Lackawanna Blues* (Executive Producer)
1999 *Introducing Dorothy Dandridge* (Executive Producer)

Halle Berry Print and Commercial Appearances
1999
TV commercial: Crispy M&Ms candy

2001
Print ads: Revlon
Television Commercial: Pepsi-Cola Twist

2000
Print ads: Revlon Super Lustrous Lipstick

2002
TNN's "James Bond for the 21st Century" (with Pierce Brosnan)

2003
Print ads: Revlon LipGlide Color Gloss Lipstick
TV commercial: Revlon Overtime Lip Colour

2004
Print ads: Army Air Force Exchange Service
Print ads: ambassador for Diabetes Aware public service campaign along with Novo Nordisk and Entertainment Industry Foundation

2006
Print ads: Versace.
Print ads: Revlon's ColorStay Makeup

2007
Print ads: Revlon's ColorStay Makeup

2008
Print ads: Revlon's ColorStay Makeup
Print ads: Revlon's ColorStay Mineral Collection color cosmetics
Print ads for Revlon's Total Definition Lash Fantasy

2009
Print ads for Revlon's Creme Gloss lipstick
Print ads for "Halle" fragrance for Halle Berry Fragrances

Music Video Appearances
1998
Appeared in the music video for Pras (former member of the Fugees): "Ghetto Supastar (That Is What You Are)" from the soundtrack for the movie *Bulworth*.

2003
Appeared in Limp Bizkit's *Behind Blue Eyes* video (from the soundtrack for the movie *Gothika*)

Other Appearances
1996
Hosted the 1996 Essence Awards (1996) with cohost/comedian Sinbad

2001
Miss November 2000 on the Maxim Uncut 2001 15-Month Calendar.

2003
TV Special: Martin Luther King Memorial Project
Punk'd (a celebrity prank show that aired on MTV, hosted by Ashton Kutchner)
host, *Saturday Night Live*, a weekly late night comedy/variety show

2008
Stand Up To Cancer, television fundraiser

2009
Host, The 40th Annual NAACP Image Awards
Presenter, Best Actress, *The 81st Annual Academy Awards*

Appendix B

SOME OF HALLE BERRY'S MAJOR AWARD WINS AND NOMINATIONS

2008

Nominated

Image Awards

Outstanding Actress in a Motion Picture for *Things We Lost in the Fire* (2007)

2007

Won

People's Choice Award

Favorite Female Action Star

2006

Won

Hasty Pudding Theatricals

Woman of the Year

Nominated

Black Movie Award

Outstanding Performance by an Actress in a Leading Role, *X-Men: The Last Stand*

Nominated

Golden Globes

Best Performance by an Actress in a Mini-Series or a Motion Picture
Made for Television for *Their Eyes Were Watching God*

Nominated
Independent Spirit Awards
Best First Feature for *Lackawanna Blues* (2005)
Shared with George C. Wolfe (director), Vince Cirrincione (producer), Ruben Santiago-Hudson (producer), Nellie Nugiel (producer), and Shelby Stone (producer)

Nominated
Outstanding Actress in a TV Movie, Mini-Series or Dramatic Special
for *Their Eyes Were Watching God*

2005
Won
Black Movie Awards
Outstanding Television Movie for *Lackawanna Blues*
Shared with Vince Cirrincione, Ruben Santiago-Hudson, Shelby
Stone, and Nellie Nugiel

Won
Golden Raspberry Award
Worst Actress, *Catwoman*

Nominated
Emmy Awards
Outstanding Made for Television Movie, *Lackawanna Blues*
Shared with Vince Cirrincione (executive producer), Shelby Stone
(executive producer), Ruben Santiago-Hudson (executive producer),
and Nellie Nugiel (producer)

Nominated
Emmy Awards
Outstanding Lead Actress in a Miniseries or a Movie, *Their Eyes Were
Watching God*

Nominated
People's Choice Award
Favorite Female Action Movie Star

Won
Razzie Award
Worst Actress, *Catwoman*

Nominated
Razzie Award
Worst Screen Couple, *Catwoman*
Shared with Benjamin Bratt and Sharon Stone

2004
Won
BET Awards
Best Actress

2003
Won
Academy Awards
Oscar, Best Actress in a Leading Role, *Monster's Ball*

Won
Image Award
Outstanding Supporting Actress in a Motion Picture for *Die Another Day*

Nominated
BAFTA Awards
Best Performance by an Actress in a Leading Role, *Monster's Ball*

2002
Nominated
AFI Film Award
AFI Actor of the Year—Female—Movies, *Monster's Ball*

Won
BET Awards
Best Actress

Won
Berlin International Film Festival
Best Actress, *Monster's Ball*

Nominated
Chicago Film Critics Association Awards
Best Actress, *Monster's Ball*

2001
Won
National Board of Review
Best Actress for *Monster's Ball*

Nominated
Golden Globe
Best Performance by an Actress in a Motion Picture—Drama, *Monster's Ball*

2000
Won
Golden Globe
Best Performance by an Actress in a Mini-Series or Motion Picture Made for TV for *Introducing Dorothy Dandridge*

Won
Emmy Award
Outstanding Lead Actress in a Miniseries or a Movie for *Introducing Dorothy Dandridge*

Nominated
Emmy Award
Outstanding Made for Television Movie for *Introducing Dorothy Dandridge* (1999)

Shared with Moctesuma Esparza (executive producer), Robert Katz (executive producer), Joshua D. Maurer (executive producer), Vince Cirrincione (executive producer), and Larry Y. Albucher

1998
Nominated
Acapulco Black Film Festival
Best Actress, *B.A.P.S.*

1997
Won
Acapulco Black Film Festival
Career Achievement Award

Won
Blockbuster Entertainment Awards
Favorite Actress—Adventure/Drama, *Executive Decision*

Won
Image Award
Outstanding Lead Actress in a Television Movie or Mini-Series for *Queen*

Image Awards
2004
- Nominated, Image Award
  Outstanding Actress in a Motion Picture for *Gothika* (2003)

2002
- Won, Image Award
  Outstanding Actress in a Motion Picture for *Swordfish* (2001)

2000
- Won, Image Award
  Outstanding Actress in a Television Movie/Miniseries/Dramatic Special for *Introducing Dorothy Dandridge* (1999)
- Special Award
  Entertainer of the Year

1999

- Nominated, Image Award
  Outstanding Lead Actress in a Motion Picture for *Bulworth* (1998)
- Nominated, Image Award
  Outstanding Lead Actress in a Television Movie or Mini-Series for *The Wedding* (1998)

1996

- Nominated, Image Award
  Outstanding Lead Actress in a Motion Picture for *Losing Isaiah* (1995)
- Nominated, Image Award
  Outstanding Actress in a Television Movie, Mini-Series for *Solomon & Sheba* (1995)

Kids' Choice Awards, USA
2007

- Nominated, Blimp Award
  Favorite Female Movie Star for *X-Men: The Last Stand* (2006)

2005

- Nominated, Blimp Award
  Favorite Movie Actress for *Catwoman* (2004)

2004

- Nominated, Blimp Award
  Favorite Movie Actress for *X2* (2003)
- Also for Gothika.

2003

- Nominated, Blimp Award
  Favorite Female Butt Kicker for *Die Another Day* (2002)

2001

- Nominated, Blimp Award
  Favorite Movie Actress for *Die Another Day* (2002)

MTV Movie Awards
2004

- Nominated, MTV Movie Award
  Best Female Performance for *Gothika* (2003)

2003

- Nominated, MTV Movie Award
  Best Female Performance for *Die Another Day* (2002)

2002

- Nominated, MTV Movie Award
  Best Female Performance for *Monster's Ball* (2001)

2001

- Nominated, MTV Movie Award
  Best On-Screen Team for *X-Men* (2000)

Shared with Hugh Jackman, James Marsden, and Anna Paquin

1995

- Nominated, MTV Movie Award
  Most Desirable Female for *The Flintstones* (1994)

1993

- Nominated, MTV Movie Award
  Best Breakthrough Performance for *Boomerang* (1992)
- Nominated, MTV Movie Award
  Most Desirable Female for *Boomerang* (1992)

People's Choice Awards, USA
2008

- Nominated, People's Choice Award
  Favorite Female Movie Star

Screen Actors Guild Awards
2002

- Won, Actor
  Outstanding Performance by a Female Actor in a Leading Role
  for *Monster's Ball* (2001)

2000

- Won, Actor
  Outstanding Performance by a Female Actor in a Television
  Movie or Miniseries for *Introducing Dorothy Dandridge* (1999)

ShoWest Convention, USA
2004

- ShoWest Award
  Female Star of the Year

Teen Choice Awards
2006
- Nominated, Teen Choice Award
  Movies—Choice Actress: Drama/Action Adventure for
  X-Men: The Last Stand (2006)

2004
- Won, Teen Choice Award
  Choice Movie Actress—Drama/Action Adventure for *Gothika*
  (2003)

2003
- Nominated, Teen Choice Award
  Choice Movie Actress—Drama/Action Adventure for *X2*
  (2003)
- Also for *Die Another Day*

Walk of Fame
April 3, 2007
- Is honored with a star on the Hollywood Walk of Fame

Women in Film Crystal Awards
2002
- Won, Crystal Award

FURTHER READING

BOOKS ABOUT HALLE BERRY

Farley, Christopher John. *Introducing Halle Berry*. Pocket Illustrated, 2002.

O'Brien, Daniel. *Halle Berry*. Reynolds & Hearn, 2003.

Sanello, Frank. *Halle Berry: A Stormy Life*. Virgin Publishing, 2004.

Schuman, Michael A. *Halle Berry: Beauty Is Not Just Physical*. Enslow Publishers, 2006.

ARTICLES BY HALLE BERRY

Berry, Halle (with Chiarella, Tom). "Halle Berry's Date with a Perfect Stranger," April 2007.

Berry, Halle. "Halle Berry Is the Sexiest Woman Alive," October 2008.

ARTICLES ABOUT HALLE BERRY

Collier, Aldore. "Why I Will Never Marry Again," *Ebony*, August 2004.

Corliss, Richard. "Halle Berry," *Time*, January 13, 2002.

Gensler, Howard. "Berry Focused," *Philadelphia Daily News*, May 24, 2006.

Jackson, Samuel L. "Halle Berry: After Ten Years, A New Kind of Breakthrough," Interview, March 2002.

Kaylin, Lucy. "Halle Berry Opens Up about 'Catwoman,' Marriage, and Life," GQ, August 2004.

Listfield, Emily. "My Sights Are Set on Motherhood," *Parade*, March 2007.

Randolph, Laura B. "Halle Berry," *Ebony*, March 1997.

Randolph, Laura B. "Halle Berry on How She Found Dorothy Dandridge's Spirit—And Finally Healed Her Own," *Ebony*, August 1999.

Touré. "Portrait of a Lady." *USA Weekend.* January 20, 2001.

Van Meter, Jonathan. "Solid Gold," *Vogue*, December 2002.

Wilson, Wendy L. "Being Halle Berry." *Essence*, March 2009.

INTERNET

Halle Berry Biography (biography.com), http://www.biography.com/articles/
Halle-Berry-9542339.

Halle Berry Fan, halleberryfan.com.

Halle Berry Photos, Bio, and News (tvguide.com), http://www.tvguide.com/
celebrities/halle-berry/152937.

Halle Berry's Official Web Site, www.hallewood.com.

Mesmerizing Halle Berry, www.halleberry.org.

INDEX

Academy Awards, 51, 62, 64–65, 72, 76, 85, 93. *See also* Oscar
Aubry, Gabriel, 87–88, 91, 94, 95–98, 102
Aubry, Nahla Abriela, 95–97, 98, 99, 100

B.A.P.S., 46–47, 49
Bassett, Angela, 36, 62–63, 66, 98
Benét, Eric, 56, 58, 59, 62, 65, 70–71, 73, 75
Benét, India, 59, 67, 70
Berry, Heidi, 2, 4, 5, 6, 7, 18
Berry, Jerome, 1–2, 4–6, 68, 72
Berry, Judith, 1–2, 4–7, 10, 18–19, 65, 66, 68, 91
Boomerang, 32–33
Brody, Adrien, 72
Bulworth, 49

car accident, 56–57, 59, 92
Catwoman, 76–79
Cirrincione, Vincent, 20, 67, 83, 110, 113
civil rights, 3
Cleveland, Ohio, 1–2, 5, 6, 16, 21, 22, 40, 41, 50, 51, 55, 68, 71

Dandridge, Dorothy, 50–53, 55–56, 79, 89, 105, 106, 112, 113, 115
diabetes, type 1, 21–23, 75–76, 95
Die Another Day, 68–70
domestic violence, 5, 6, 8, 34, 35, 68, 71

Ealy, Michael, 86
Executive Decision, 45

Father Hood, 35
Flintstones, The, 42–43
Forster, Marc, 59, 60, 61, 67, 84, 101. *See also Monster's Ball*

Goldberg, Whoopi, 64–65
Gothika, 74–75

Haley, Alex, 33. *See also Queen*
Halle Brothers Department Store, 1
"Halle by Halle Berry" perfume, 96, 100
Hollywood Walk of Fame, 90–91

Interracial marriage, 3
Introducing Dorothy Dandridge, 55, 58, 89

Jackman, Hugh, 63
Jackson, Samuel L., 27, 28, 41, 91
Jungle Fever, 27–30, 36, 61
Justice, David, 39–41, 43, 44–45,
    46, 56

Knots Landing, 26–27

Lackawanna Blues, 83–84
Last Boy Scout, The, 30, 31
Lee, Spike, 27–28, 61, 67
Living Dolls, 20–22, 75, 106
Losing Isaiah, 41–42

Miss Ohio, 15
Miss Teen Ohio, 9, 15
Miss USA Pageant, 15
Miss World Pageant, 15–16
modeling, 20, 21, 23, 25, 50, 70,
    88, 96
Monster's Ball, 61–67, 79, 84, 92, 101

Oakwood Village, Ohio, 5–6
Obama, Barack, 95, 102
Oscar, 31, 59, 65–67, 71, 76, 79, 85,
    89, 94

Perfect Stranger, 91–92
Program, The, 35
prom queen, 9–10

Queen, 33–35

Race the Sun, 45–46
Razzie Awards, 79
Revlon, 50, 70, 97, 102
Rich Man's Wife, The, 45, 46
Robots, 85
Ronan, John, 20, 22

Solomon and Sheba, 44
stalker, 72–74
Strictly Business, 30
suicide contemplated, 19, 46, 71
Swordfish, 63–64

Their Eyes Were Watching God,
    85–86
Things We Lost in the Fire, 92–93
Thornton, Billy Bob, 60, 62, 63,
    67, 87

Versace, 87

Why Do Fools Fall in Love, 49–50
Winfrey, Oprah, 48, 68

X-Men, 58, 63, 72, 76, 89
X-Men 2, 72–73, 76
X-Men: The Last Stand, 90

ABOUT THE AUTHOR

MELISSA EWEY JOHNSON is a former editor at *Ebony* magazine. Her writing has appeared in various publications in print and online, including *Essence, Heart & Soul, Honey, Real Health, Woman's Day,* and *Fitness*. She lives with her husband in New York City.